ZOO BOOK

The Evolution of Wildlife Conservation Centers

LINDA KOEBNER

PREFACE BY WILLIAM CONWAY
GENERAL DIRECTOR
WILDLIFE CONSERVATION SOCIETY

A Forge Hardcover

A Tom Doherty Associates Book
New York

ZOO BOOK

This book is printed on acid-free paper.

A Forge Book
Published by Tom Doherty Associates, Inc.
175 Fifth Avenue
New York, N.Y. 10010

Designed by
Jennifer Blanc/Neuwirth & Associates

Library of Congress Cataloging-in-Publication Data
Koebner, Linda.
Zoo book: the evolution of wildlife   conservation
centers/Linda Koebner.
p. cm.
ISBN 0-312-85322-X
1. Zoos. 2. Zoos --North America. I Title.
QL76.K63 1994
590' .74'4 --dc20
94-121
CIP

First Edition: June 1994

Printed in the United States of America

0   9   8   7   6   5   4   3   2   1

The zoos and individuals highlighted in *Zoo Book*
were selected as representations and examples for the
whole. In no way does this reflect the merit of any one
person, zoo, or project. Wildlife and conservation efforts
are constantly changing. Every effort was made to have
accurate facts and figures at the time the
manuscript went to press.

ZOO BOOK

The Evolution of Wildlife Conservation Centers

For Omi ...my grandmother
Helmuth, Ben and Ruth...her children
and Ian my son....
Over a century of special memories from
time shared in zoos worldwide.
May the efforts of conservation centers today
make it possible for Ian's grandchildren
to experience the continued evolution and
splendor of wildlife—in the wild.

Contents

SECTION III. LOOKING TO THE FUTURE

"In our every deliberation,
we must consider the impact of
our decisions on the next
seven generations."

—From *the Great Law
of the Iroquois Confederacy*

Acknowledgments

Scores of people who have touched my life over the past forty years, influenced this book. I thank all of them for what they have taught me about the human capability to care for nature, as well as pointing out to me how some people have a total disregard for life.

Zoos touch a cord in people—they have for centuries. But now more than ever they bring up strong emotions—for or against. This project made me take a very close look at zoos today and how they have evolved over the centuries as a reflection of the evolution of the human relationship to non-human animals.

There are still many people who exploit animals, but a growing number cherish them and work to secure their place in the world with us. Many of those people work for zoos, inside the walls and beyond them, to conserve wildlife. Yet it is the public, all of us, the 100.8 million people of the United States who love to visit the zoo every year, who must expect a certain standard of care for the animals. We can no longer expect only to be entertained at the zoo. The definition is changing once again, as it has over centuries.

I have been fortunate to visit many zoos both in the United States and worldwide. I have cared for animals in captivity and observed them in the wild. I have worked with individuals who are opposed to zoos as well as with those who promote their work.

The evolution of my acknowledgments:

Thanks to the committed and caring individuals of the Wildlife Conservation Society, where I learned firsthand about the creation and the inner workings of a zoo.

A special thank-you to Dr. George Schaller, who opened the Rainey Gate for me—allowing me a vision of the zoo from within.

William Conway, General Director of the Wildlife Conservation Society, who inspires everyone with his knowledge, dedication and ability to know what to do in the best interest of wildlife.

Richard Lattis, who gave me the opportunity to work alongside him, and was a wonderful mentor. The depth of his knowledge is almost as vast as his good humor, kindness, and ability to pull a million pieces together into a magnificent whole.

A special thanks to Catherine Belden... her spirit and ability are remarkable. To Peter Glankoff for his support and belief in the project. Thanks to Martha Schwartz for always being there for me and for her amazing ability to know how to reach everyone and everything.

Many others in the Society have been

important to me in my life and in thinking about this book. I thank them for consistently being warm and welcoming no matter how many years have passed.

If I missed anyone, I apologize, there are so many individuals who have helped me... among them:

Debbie Behler	Anthony Marshall
John Behler, Jr.	Denise McClean
Annette Berkokvitz	Luann McGrain
James J. Breheny	John McKew
Donald Bruning	Geoffrey Mellor
Chuck Carr	Bill Meng
Linda Corcoran	Patricia Moehlman
Ellen Dierenfeld	Charles Munn
Dennis DeMello	Mary Pearl
James Doherty	Alan Rabinowitz
Judy Dufflemeyer	John G. Robinson
Carole Ferster	Stuart Strahl
Don Goddard	Christine Sheppard
Sheila Goldberg	Judy Unis
Nancy Granchelli	Amy Vedder
John Gwynne	Tom Veltre
John Hoare	Virginia Walsh
Louise Ingenito	Bill Webber
Steven Johnson	Wendy Westrom
William Karesh	Dan Wharton
Fred Koontz	Helena Zengara
Sharon Kramer	

Everyone from the admission gatekeeper to zoo instructors, photographers, secretaries, keepers of the commissaries, directors, keepers, ethologists, writers of articles, and the thousands of visitors I have observed...all contributed to this book.

Many other zoos, organizations, and individuals have given generously of their time, thoughts, research, and criticism. Thanks to everyone who spoke to me between sessions at AZA meetings, on the phone, or on walks through the zoo.

Special thanks to Sydney Butler for the vision and energy he is bringing to the AZA, and the time he has given to this project. Thanks also to Robert J. Wiese, and Michael Hutchins, who worked so long and with such studied care on the manuscript. To Jane Ballentine, Bob Ramin at the AZA, and to David Jenkins, Karen Assis and Nancy Hotchkiss for their help while they were there. Nancy, always the nucleus of the complex zoo universe, sparked this project with her enthusiasm; never knowing what wonderful version of a welcome I would get on the other end of the line, but always a cheerful one.

Dr. George Rabb, Director of the Brookfield Zoo, generously allowed me to use his zoo evolution chart, which illustrates so perfectly where they have been and where they are going. He is a stellar example of a man who cares about the future of the planet and all its inhabitants...and acts on his convictions with energy and thoughtfulness.

Terry Maple, Director of Zoo Atlanta, has always been an inspiration to me. His understanding of the great apes has, I am certain, contributed to his excellent achievements within the zoo walls and outside of them. His welcome is always warm and his encouragement meant the world to me.

I thank all the other zoo directors who shared their knowledge and time with me: Y. Sherry Sheng, Metro Washington Park Zoo, Thomas C. Otten, Point Defiance Zoo, Palmer Kranz, Riverbanks Zoo, Ron Forman, Audubon Park and Zoo, Patricia Simmons, Akron Zoo, David Hancocks at The Arizona-Sonora Desert Museum, Warren Illif, Phoenix Zoo, Kevin Bell, the Lincoln Park Zoo.

Robert C. Lacey, Cynthia Vernon and Amy Samuels shared their knowledge. I have been fortunate to know Amy over the years, as she has brought her dedication from dolphins to chimpanzees and back to dolphins again.

Bob Johnson and Toby Styles at the Metro Toronto Zoo; Bob Hoage, and Chris Wemmer, Ben Beck, Devra Kleinman and Kathy Carlstead at the National Zoo.

Jeff Jouett, San Diego Zoo, Wilbur Amand, Philadelphia Zoo, and Sandy Skrei; Betsy Dresser, Vicki, and Thane Maynard, Cincinnati Zoo; Ken Kawata, Steve Johnson, and Vernon Kisling, who patiently helped me with zoo history; David Shepardson, who is enriching many lives.

Ulysses Seal and Nathan Flesness, Executive Director, ISIS, who had a remarkable vision and managed to make it an orderly reality. Gay Rheinhard, who cares so much for bonobos, and all the SSP coordinators who gave generously of information, photographs and of their own time to try and save species.

The keepers who walked me "behind the scenes" and everyone who gave of their photography collections.

Jon Coe and Dave and Jonquil Rock, who are able to transform respect for nature into works of art. Thanks for helping me get a better understanding of how you do it. Jon gave unwaveringly of his time, ideas, and experience, always there and ready to help. Always able to see things just a bit more clearly. Thank you.

Jane Goodall, Bob Edison and Virginia Landau at the Jane Goodall Institute. Patti Forkan, you have been there over the years as who we are and what we do evolves—always a friend. Steven Zawistowski, Roger Caras, Mike Kaufman, John Grandy, all working towards the same end.

Cathy Bell, who was really there for me and for this project. Thanks for helping me out of my vacuum with your openness, your experience, and wonderful enthusiasm.

All the field biologists, who I envy and admire—especially to Linda Marchant and Bill McGrew, who prove beyond a doubt that things do work out the way they are supposed to.

My gracious hosts at the Copenhagen Zoo, Hagenbeck Zoo, Frankfurt Zoo and Berlin Zoo.

And where would this book be without Kathleen Doherty? Her thoughtfulness, diligence, and view of what this could be. Fortunately, the book took time because our friendship grew along with the words. Thanks to Linda Quinton for her wonderful spirit, always buoying me up. And to Tom Doherty for how well he nurtured his daughters. And thanks to Barbara Bova for bringing us all together.

Special thanks to Stefan Gerard for making certain that things got done in his calm and optimistic way and thanks to Jenny Blanc for working so hard to bring the words alive by presenting them so beautifully.

Thanks is only the edge of what to say to my family, Ian, Mummy, and Hans, for their love and support during my own evolution, and to Ron with joy that our evolution continues.

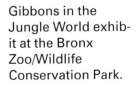

Gibbons in the Jungle World exhibit at the Bronx Zoo/Wildlife Conservation Park.

Preface
by William Conway

🐎

"**A**nimal collections," "menageries" and "zoological gardens" are names that reflect human curiosity about the animal kingdom throughout history. Until recent decades, however, that interest was rarely matched by understanding or concern for the animals' well-being.

The recent evolution of zoos reflects our changing insight into the interdependence of the human species with all other species, and our increasing awareness of the accelerating environmental crisis threatening the earth's natural ecosystems and animal populations.

Zoos have become central in advancing science, technology and management—areas that are essential to preserving the earth's natural ecological diversity.

Equally important, however, is the implementation of a broad-based and far-reaching educational agenda that successfully communicates the importance of biodiversity and the severity of the extinction crisis with which we are faced. Only with a widely based and deeply felt concern for environmental and animal protection will there be the necessary financial and political support to implement large-scale, long-range environmental conservation projects in nature.

It is with this broad mission in mind that the New York Zoological Society, after 100 years of leadership in wildlife science and preservation, changed its name to the Wildlife Conservation Society. Since its formation in 1895, the organization and its zoos have been steadfast in their commitment to wildlife conservation in their parks and through field projects, largely ignoring the names and nicknames created by visitors, the media and our own employees.

Early in the century, one of my predecessors, William T. Hornaday, railed against newspapers who referred to the "New York Zoo," or the "Zoo Society." He insisted on "Zoological" and "Park," and wrote letters to that effect to all sixteen daily newspapers in the city. Bronx Zoo was shorter and stuck. Evolution is slow.

But our dedication to the conservation of wildlife did not change over the century. We went on working harder, seeking to achieve the survival of wildlife as problems became more complex.

For us, the work "zoo" conveys a narrow image of the menageries of yesteryear, not of the six wild animal expositions and breeding centers we operate today. It gives no idea of the Society's extensive research in conservation science and propagation of vanishing species, its 200 direct programs of ecosystem preservation around the developing world and its environmental education programs. Today, we are most simply and deeply a wildlife conservation society. And the "Bronx Zoo," which will probably always be with us, has become the Wildlife Conservation Park. We are not alone. The accredited zoos of the 1990s are a nationwide and worldwide network working cooperatively to the same end. Many zoos are evolving into conservation centers.

Zoos seemed destined to become living museums of natural history—places where future generations, if they bothered to venture away from the wildlife specials on tape or digital tracks, might come to see relics of a world that once was.

That was until recently, when the institutions and their employees have taken a more active role. They are served by scientific technology, a greater understanding of animal behavior and a clear view that the severity of the threat to the biosphere requires the best efforts of all concerned—professional and public.

With over 800 million visitors annually, the world's 1,100 zoos and aquariums are among our society's greatest and longest-running recreational attractions. As their role has changed, conservation centers are evermore the best bet for involving you, the visiting public, in preserving the earth's natural bounty and diversity.

Zoo Book, The Evolution of Wildlife Conservation Centers is an interesting, insightful and comprehensive introduction into the history, philosophy and inner workings of zoos—written and illustrated for people of all ages and backgrounds. It is an important contribution to the critical educational efforts now underway.

William Conway

General Director

Wildlife Conservation Society

"We stand guard over works of
art, but species representing the
work of eons are stolen from
under our noses."

—*Aldo Leopold*

"This being the only living
world we are ever likely
to know, let us join to make
the most of it."

—*E. O. Wilson*

Introduction

The woman crouches on the steep, forested hillside, partially hidden by thick nettles. Her thigh has a fierce cramp, but she doesn't dare shift her weight to stretch her leg. She doesn't dare move. A gorilla mother approaches through the vegetation and sits just ten feet away. She settles her infant on her lap and begins nursing him. An older brother stumbles into view, dragging a branch. The woman holds her breath, both hoping and fearing that the gorilla family will see her. She has been waiting a long time.

An icy stillness permeates the white-tiled room rimmed by cabinets, counters and bottles. Light floods the steel six-foot operating table. Ten worried faces gaze down from the balcony of the operating theater. With three assistants looking on, the anesthesiologist nods at the doctor. The doctor takes a deep breath and makes the first cut with his scalpel, trying to save the rare Siberian tiger.

As different as they are, both these scenes pertain to the modern mission of zoos.

We are entering an exciting new time for zoos. Our relationship to the entire animal kingdom is changing as quickly as we gain knowledge. We hope we are learning and changing fast enough. We have to hurry or it will be too late to preserve the animal kingdom as we know it. The excitement comes from knowing that we can make a difference in these life-and-death matters—in fact, we must make a difference. Countries, organizations and individual people are working together for the same thing—to save and protect animals. And zoos are becoming ever more central in the effort.

As much of the world's wildlife disappears, knowledgeable humans must use their skills both in the zoo and around the world if many of the earth's species are to survive.

By now, in the 1990s, we have learned an enormous amount about wildlife, but still not enough. We have only begun to understand animal behavior and how the web of life is strung. As fast as we discover previously unknown species, countless others disappear, become extinct. We have learned that the supply of animals is not endless, as we once thought. In fact, we are learning the hard way that they, like all of the earth's resources, are limited.

If a crucial balance of the earth's wildlife is to survive, if someday we hope to return animals faced with extinction to their natural habitats, then we must take action now. We rush to learn about the behavior of gorillas, just ahead of the encroachment of human guerrillas for their own living space. We race to finish studies of life in the rain forest before the chain saw sends trees and their secrets crashing down.

Since humans first held wild animals in captivity, zoos have evolved through many phases. Regrettably, though, there are still far too many zoos that resemble the menageries of the Middle Ages, holding animals inhumanely in cramped cages with no regard for their natural needs. In the twentieth century, these zoos are a disgrace and should not exist. Many people fight every day to change these horrors.

Beyond how it exhibits the animals, the best measures of the quality of a zoo are how well the animals are cared for, how it contributes to conservation and, of great importance, what it teaches about wildlife. The best zoos are centers of learning for biologists, geneticists and veterinarians, as well as the public.

There are many zoos that provide good care and meet their missions of conservation, education and research but have not yet moved completely to the next evolutionary state: zoos as conservation centers. That is the aim. In fact, recently several zoos were renamed "Wildlife Conservation Centers." It may take some time for people to get used to calling them that, or to fully understand their modern mission, or for even the best zoos to have only the best possible exhibits. In the meantime, zoos will continue to educate the public about the importance of protecting ecosystems and the importance of wildlife.

Today, zoos are providing a home not only for unusual wild animals but for animals that are extinct in the wild. Zoos are doing their work not only within their walls but outside, assisting people worldwide to protect the animals and the land they need. Zoos are setting up wildlife preserves so that entire ecosystems can be protected.

Once, zoos were only for the powerful and the rich, for important guests to visit. Today, the animals in zoos are our important guests.

In *Zoo Book*, you will read about the way zoos were and the way they are going to be.

Rhinoceros and sable antelope at the San Diego Wild Animal Park

"In the end, we will conserve
only what we love.
We will love only what we
understand. We will
understand what we are
taught."

—*Baba Dioum,*
Senegalese conservationist

Section I
Zoos Around the Continent

Chapter One
ZOOS AROUND THE CONTINENT

Each of the 162 AZA (American Zoo and Aquarium Association)-accredited North American zoos is unique in its appearance, its animals and its management. It is possible that within the next twenty years, many zoos will be called "conservation centers," the name for the next stage of their evolution. But, for the remainder of this book, all accredited collections of animals will be referred to as zoos.

Like the National Zoo in Washington, D.C., some have a very long history. Others, like the WILDS in Columbus, Ohio, were created very recently. There are zoos exhibiting many species of animals or just a few. Some are tiny—in the heart of a city—and others cover hundreds of acres.

A zoo can be owned by the city, in which case it is municipal. It can be managed by a zoological society or it can be privately owned by an individual, a company, a family or a combination of these.

SAN DIEGO WILD ANIMAL PARK
San Diego, California
Opened 1972

The San Diego Wild Animal Park, thirty miles north of downtown San Diego, is an example of a zoo dedicated to displaying animals in large, naturalistic exhibits. Designed first for the animals and second for the people who come to see them, it is a park of 2,150 acres where herds of animals can roam in vast enclosures, with dirt and grass under their feet.

When the San Diego Wild Animal Park opened to the public, zoos were beginning to focus more on conservation. The park was designed to be a sanctuary for wildlife. Currently, it is home to about 1,000 mammals and 1,800 birds. The San Diego Zoo and the Wild Animal Park also provide a place for thousands of rare plants. The park prides itself on being a successful research and breeding facility; of the fifty endangered species protected at the park, thirty-nine have been bred

and have given birth to healthy babies. These include pygmy chimpanzees, Sumatran tigers, South African cheetahs, East African black rhinos, Przewalski's horses, Indian gaurs, California condors and Bali mynahs. Many hoof stock need to be in herds for the right conditions to mate and produce young. At the San Diego Wild Animal Park, there is space for the animals to be in large herds, the right environment for them to breed.

A major advantage of the San Diego Wild Animal Park is that the climate of southern California is much like that of the African plains, the original home of many of the park's animals. The animals can be outside year-round, making many buildings unnecessary. In fact, only the more sensitive species—gorillas, okapi, tigers, chimps and cheetahs—are "put up" in pens or buildings at night for their safety and warmth. The other animals can be outside all the time.

The zoo has very good research facilities. Students and scientists study the animals in a natural situation without going into the wild. In fact, over forty percent of the park is only for the animals—off limits to visitors. This area is kept for breeding facilities for the California condor and the cheetah and for various behavioral and reproductive research projects.

As soon as you go through the admission gates into the San Diego Wild Animal Park, you are transported to a world far removed from the traffic and housing developments along the highway from the city of San Diego to the park.

The transition suggests that you have entered a village in the east African country of Kenya. You walk through a flight cage, a huge aviary resembling a natural environ-

Lagoon view of San Diego Wild Animal Park.

ment. In the flight cage are bridged ponds, trees, flowers and the rich damp smell of dark soil and ferns. In this village, with its thatched roofs, you will walk past exhibits of monkeys, gorillas and gazelles (and maybe more souvenir and refreshment stands than you would like, but zoos have to find ways to pay for themselves).

Then you can opt either to ride the monorail or to walk the path that leads to overlooks of the African plains and through the Australian rain forest, where you will see animals native to Australia, such as kookaburras and kangaroos.

The San Diego Wild Animal Park invites all fifth graders of the San Diego area on a visit. School programs are open to all classes K–12, but this special program introduces the children to what has caused endangered species and the environmental problems fac-

ing all of us. At the park, they can see the animals firsthand.

The monorail, or Wagasa Bush Line (all the areas of the park have African names), is a five-mile, fifty-minute ride around the perimeter of the park. It glides quietly past the large herds of grazing African animals, which are sometimes tussling for territory or mates as they might on the African plains.

When the day cools off, the wildlife of the African plains becomes active. From the hillKside, you can see a group of ten giraffes lope across the veld, or wide grassy plain. The young ones, all legs, chase each other around the adults. They stop quickly when two rhinos walk through their space. The rhinos pay no attention to the youngsters, their eyesight so poor that they can't see clearly more than six feet ahead. The giraffes keep a respectful distance, in case the quick-tempered rhinos

Giraffes at sunset at the San Diego Wild Animal Park.

Pygmy Chimpanzee

This relatively unkown primate has great similarities to man. And these incredibly intelligent, social animals may soon become extinct. The pygmy chimpanzee, also called "bonobo," is the rarest of all ape species. In the wild, it is only found in central Zaire in Africa. We ordinarily think of the common chimpanzee as the great ape that most resembles its relatives, human beings. But perhaps the pygmy chimpanzee is even more hauntingly like us in behavior, intellect and body structure. In the wild, pygmy chimps may be gone by the end of the century. The San Diego Wild Animal Park is one of the facilities that cares for the eighty-five animals known to exist in captivity worldwide.

East African Black Rhino

In just seventeen years, Kenya, Africa, lost ninety-eight percent of its black rhinos. The population went from an estimated 19,999 in 1970 to fewer than 400 in 1987. They are killed for their horns, which are believed to give great power as an aphrodisiac; the horns are powdered to be taken as a tonic or they are carved into daggers. Often poachers kill the rhino and cut away the horn, leaving the body to rot and be eaten by vultures and other scavengers. Great efforts are being made to protect the black rhino by setting up preserves in Africa and bringing global attention to the horrors of their extinction.

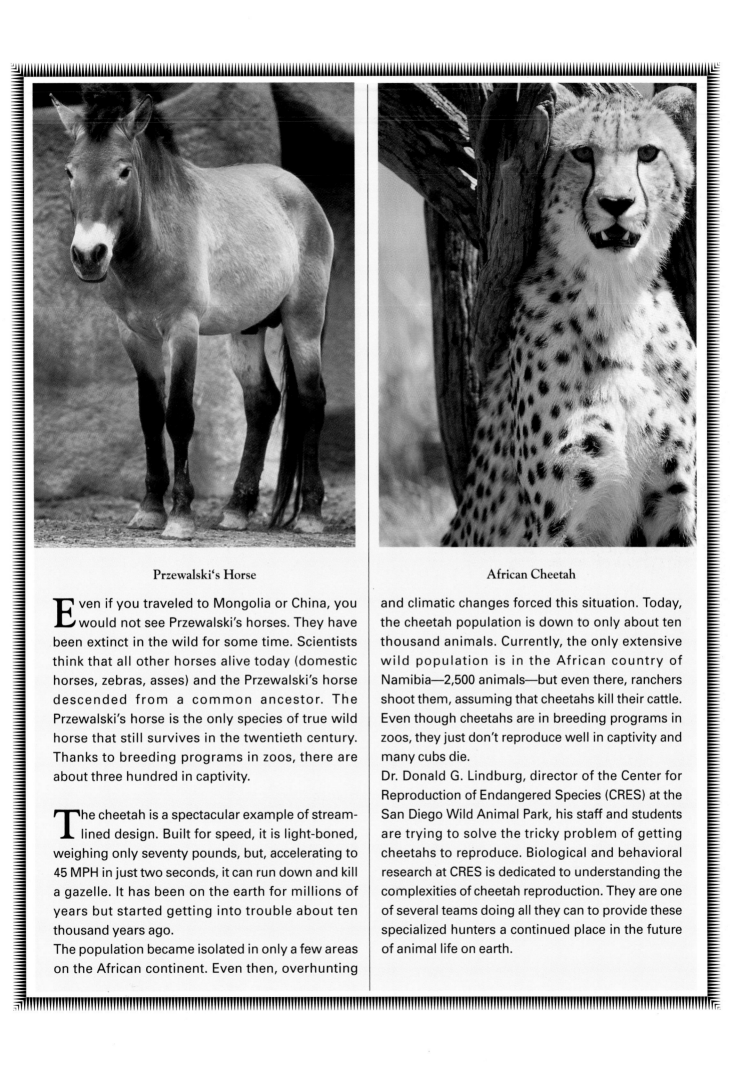

Przewalski's Horse

African Cheetah

Even if you traveled to Mongolia or China, you would not see Przewalski's horses. They have been extinct in the wild for some time. Scientists think that all other horses alive today (domestic horses, zebras, asses) and the Przewalski's horse descended from a common ancestor. The Przewalski's horse is the only species of true wild horse that still survives in the twentieth century. Thanks to breeding programs in zoos, there are about three hundred in captivity.

The cheetah is a spectacular example of stream-lined design. Built for speed, it is light-boned, weighing only seventy pounds, but, accelerating to 45 MPH in just two seconds, it can run down and kill a gazelle. It has been on the earth for millions of years but started getting into trouble about ten thousand years ago.

The population became isolated in only a few areas on the African continent. Even then, overhunting and climatic changes forced this situation. Today, the cheetah population is down to only about ten thousand animals. Currently, the only extensive wild population is in the African country of Namibia—2,500 animals—but even there, ranchers shoot them, assuming that cheetahs kill their cattle. Even though cheetahs are in breeding programs in zoos, they just don't reproduce well in captivity and many cubs die.

Dr. Donald G. Lindburg, director of the Center for Reproduction of Endangered Species (CRES) at the San Diego Wild Animal Park, his staff and students are trying to solve the tricky problem of getting cheetahs to reproduce. Biological and behavioral research at CRES is dedicated to understanding the complexities of cheetah reproduction. They are one of several teams doing all they can to provide these specialized hunters a continued place in the future of animal life on earth.

In 1992, the San Diego Wild Animal Park opened a hummingbird aviary and filled it with 600–700 magnificently colored butterflies from butterfly farms in Costa Rica, helping the population in Costa Rica continue a business. The butterfly farm is one of a growing number of "sustainable" businesses developing in tropical countries. These businesses, which include growing native plants like the Brazil nuts used in Ben & Jerry's Rain Forest Crunch ice cream flavor, help the local people while protecting trees. Year after year, there will be nuts as well as butterflies if these programs succeed.

decide to charge at a leaf blowing by and swipe at them by mistake. Nearby, Thompson gazelles graze, chomping off the tips of fresh grass. A vulture perches on a hollow tree overlooking the plain and sits quietly watching the scene.

This view into the wild, provided at the San Diego Wild Animal Park, is one not likely to be experienced without travel to Africa, Asia or Australia.

The San Diego Wild Animal Park has a commitment to conservation of species and the environment, both locally and internationally.

ARIZONA-SONORA DESERT MUSEUM
Tucson, Arizona
Opened 1952

The Arizona-Sonora Desert Museum (ASDM) displays indigenous wildlife, presenting a slice of the vast Sonora Desert landscape in a way that reveals its richness. It educates on the entire ecosystem, both the living (plant and animal life) and the inert (geology, climate and history).

The ASDM does not have animals from distant lands; rather, it exhibits only animals that live naturally in the surrounding Sonora Desert, one of four deserts on the North American continent (the Great Basin, the Mojave and the Chihuahuan are the other three).

The ASDM is just outside of Tucson. It is not readily discernible from a distance because it blends into the landscape. The ASDM was founded to promote understanding of this desert.

The founders, Arthur N. Pack and William H. Carr, considered education to be the first step to conservation. They believed that if people understood the complexity and beauty of the desert, they would be more likely to protect it. Deserts are often perceived as desolate, arid sand where scant life exists, with no value beyond perhaps as a potential commercial

Arizona-Sonora Desert Museum, view of Cactus Garden.

Top: Earth Science cave formation—man-made from wire, rods, and Gunite.

Bottom: Mineral display in Earth Science Center.

development site. Yet the desert, like any other ecosystem, is filled with a diversity of life and is fragile and must be treated with great care.

The Sonora Desert for the most part is low, hot and dry, with summer temperatures reaching 120°F and humidity often less than ten percent. But it also reaches into the mountains of Arizona and Sonora, Mexico, and extends along the coastline of Baja California. What defines it as a desert is that the rate of water evaporation exceeds the amount of rainfall, which is less than ten inches annually.

The Sonora Desert covers about 120,000 square miles and hosts many more plant and animal species than most other deserts in the world. The ASDM contains more than 1,200 species of plants and 200 species of live animals in enclosures that imitate their natural habitats. The ASDM is 186 acres, but so far

only fifteen are developed. Still, the ASDM explains the entire ecosystem and how the land, plants and animals are interrelated.

Before coming upon most of the animal exhibits, the visitor may enter a dark limestone cave with a winding, narrow path that seems to have been carved over the centuries. But this "limestone" is new, a combination of wire, rods and Gunite (a kind of cement) sculpted and painted to look like the real thing. It even fools the animals. Bats sometimes spend time hanging upside down in the cave, and a king snake once spent a great deal of time coming and going through the drainage holes.

The visitor emerges from the cave into a huge room where the past 4.5 billion years are explained—the earth from its beginning as a planet. The display of minerals in the Earth Science Center is among the most exquisite in the world. The ASDM interprets the commu-

nities found within the Sonora Desert or alongside it: the mountain islands, the desert grasslands or desert riparian areas. Soon a tropical deciduous forest will be added to explain the evolution of Sonora Desert plants and animals.

Naturalistic exhibits are home to animals of the area: black bear, beaver, otter, bighorn sheep and many members of the cat family. Many of these cats are rarely seen in the wild, in part because so many have been killed for their beautiful coats, and in part because most cats are nocturnal, hunting at night.

The Arizona-Sonora Desert Museum opens visitors' eyes to this one place in the world, bringing the richness of nature up close: feeling the rush of a Costa's hummingbird's wings near your cheek, seeing how the desert mice build cities, watching the black bears wrestle or examining the diversity of rock and cacti.

Bobcat in natural setting at the Arizona-Sonora Desert Museum.

THE LINCOLN PARK ZOO
Chicago, Illinois
Opened 1886

The Lincoln Park Zoo is an example of a municipal zoo. It is in partnership with the city; the expenses, upkeep, food and care for the 1,800 exotic animals are shared by the city and the Zoological Society. Lincoln Park Zoo is on public land, and the Parks Department is the city agency of Chicago responsible for it.

This zoo is designed taxonomically, meaning the exhibits are grouped by the taxonomic group or kind of animal on display: the primate house, the bird house, the reptile house and so on. For over a century, the Lincoln Park Zoo has provided excellent animal care, has been a leader in exhibit design and has had an excellent record of breeding endangered animals—all in a tiny zoo in the middle of a huge city. It is an example of a zoo which has been able to evolve with change, from menagerie to contemporary exhibit design.

The Lincoln Park Zoo is one of the best-attended zoos in the country. It is open every day of the year and is free of charge. Each year, the Lincoln Park Zoo has an estimated several million visitors. Young families, couples, visitors to the city, senior citizens and busloads of school children visit the Lincoln Park Zoo.

Of all the AZA-accredited zoos, almost half are municipal zoos, which are generally thirty-six percent smaller than others. The average size is 75 acres as opposed to 115 acres for private zoos. Generally, the numbers of animals and personnel, and the amount of money the city provides, are smaller for a municipal zoo than for a private zoo.

Although Lincoln Park is mostly funded by the city, like many other municipal zoos, there is a zoological society associated with it. Today, zoological societies may help with fund-raising for special projects or take responsibility for certain parts of the zoo, like the education department. The zoological society can help provide money that the city cannot afford. At the Lincoln Park Zoo, the

Top: View of Large Animal House, Lincoln Park Zoo, about 1900.

Bottom: View of Lincoln Park Zoo now.

Zoological Society, which was founded in 1959, continues to work hard on conservation programs. Since 1975, the society has raised $55 million to enhance the zoo's work.

As one of the oldest zoos in the country, in the same spot since 1868, the Lincoln Park Zoo is a blend of the old and the new, an oasis tucked in a beautiful corner of a contemporary city on the edge of Lake Michigan.

Many of the early stately and ornate buildings your great-grandparents would have seen remain. The bird house, the lion house and the primate house were all built between 1904 and 1911. The builders of the time worked with great detail. Several of the buildings have splendid mosaics and handcrafted tiles circling the walls. The zoo looks old from the outside, yet inside are modern-day exhibits.

At one time, the Brach Primate House had thirty-one tiny menagerie-like cages with a huge gallery space for the visitors—an allocation of space that is a good example of priorities in the early days of zoos. Now, after renovation, inside the same walls there are

Left: Outside of the McCormick Bird House, built in 1904.

Right: Inside the McCormick Bird House, 1993—a free-flight tropical forest exhibit.

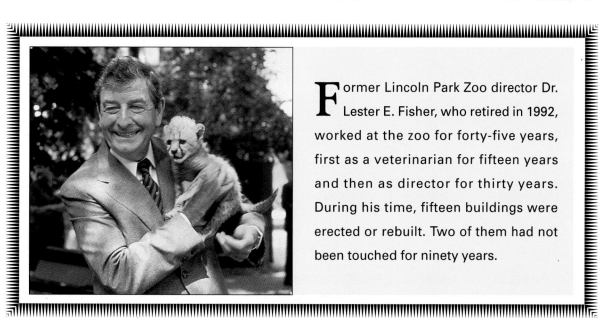

Former Lincoln Park Zoo director Dr. Lester E. Fisher, who retired in 1992, worked at the zoo for forty-five years, first as a veterinarian for fifteen years and then as director for thirty years. During his time, fifteen buildings were erected or rebuilt. Two of them had not been touched for ninety years.

eight enclosures. One huge outdoor space stretches the entire length of the building. Instead of being in cramped, barren cages, the primates have nine spacious, naturalistic enclosures. The visitors' space is comfortable, but limited.

The same kind of transformation has taken place in the McCormick Bird House, where cages have been reduced from fifty to nine, and in the Lion House, where twenty-six box-like cages have been reduced to ten habitats. With these architectural changes, the Lincoln Park Zoo illustrates neatly the evolution of America's zoos.

As the Lincoln Park Zoo moved away from the postage stamp style, it began to focus on breeding programs for several species, including the lowland gorilla and the Bali mynah, a highly endangered bird. Recently, an Asian elephant was born in the zoo.

Historically, gorillas have not done well in zoos. No other zoo in the country has been as successful in breeding western lowland gorillas. Since 1970, thirty-eight gorillas have been born at Lincoln Park, fifteen percent of captive gorilla births in North America. Lincoln Park Zoo has now been able to provide a situation in which the gorillas do breed and produce healthy babies, but it did not start out that way. It had been an example of the way most great apes were kept early in American zoo history.

There are three subspecies of gorilla: mountain, western lowland and eastern lowland. Although we hear more about the critically endangered status of mountain gorillas, there are none presently in zoos. They have always been in very remote areas, high in the Virunga Mountains shared by the African nations of Zaire, Rwanda and Uganda. Two taken into captivity in the early seventies died. Since then, their endangered status prohibits them from being captured and removed from their natural habitat. Fortunately, with tighter controls on hunting and the establishment of reserves, their population is stable. The gorillas you see in zoos are usually western lowland gorillas, whose habitat ranges over western Africa.

Since their habitat is more accessible to humans, infant lowland gorillas have been readily captured and traded, so they appeared early on in menageries, circuses and zoos. They number about forty thousand in the wild. The eastern lowland gorilla, whose habitat is in eastern Zaire, numbers only about five thousand, and perhaps as low as two thousand. There are only about a dozen in captivity.

Until recently, western lowland gorillas have not been very successful breeders in zoos.

In 1931, the first gorilla arrived at the Lincoln Park Zoo from Africa. Named Bushman, he was two years old and weighed thirty-eight pounds. At his death in 1951, he was six feet tall and weighed 550 pounds. In keeping with the times, he was exhibited alone in a cage for twenty years, his entire lifetime. People came to see the scary monster image of King Kong.

Left: The Brach Primate House as it was originally built. Sterile cages were the primary means of exhibiting animals for many years.

Right: Renovated Brach Primate House. Immersion exhibits are the primary means of exhibit.

Fortunately for the captive lowland gorilla population, this trend did not last. People came to understand that gorillas are social animals and need companionship. Otto, who came to the zoo in 1968, became father to fifteen babies. Like Bushman, he was a favorite for the visitors, but for very different reasons. Otto, in a social setting, allowed the public to see an adult male gorilla as he really is, a gentle, nurturing part of a family, not a monster.

When Kumba was born in 1970, he became the first of the continuing dynasty of gorillas at the Lincoln Park Zoo. Six of the first seven births at the zoo were females—a lucky occurrence for the gorillas of Lincoln Park Zoo. Since the natural composition of a gorilla troop is one dominant male (the "silverback"), several females and their children, more females meant that the troop could stay together. If there had been more males, they would have had to be moved as they became adults. The gorilla colony grew quickly into three separate troops. In fact, Lincoln Park lowland gorillas bred so well that an entire

Bushman, a western lowland gorilla. Bushman was the first gorilla to arrive at the Lincoln Park Zoo in 1931. Bushman was two years old and weighed thirty-eight pounds on his arrival. At his death in 1951 he was six feet tall and 550 pounds. Keeping with the times he was exhibited alone in a cage for twenty years. Now, at the Lincoln Park Zoo you can see whole families of lowland gorillas living together.

Kumba, offspring of Otto, born in 1970, became the first of the continuing dynasty of lowand gorillas at the Lincoln Park Zoo.

troop was taken to the St. Louis Zoo when they opened an exhibit.

Why has the gorilla population done so well at Lincoln Park Zoo? Part luck and part good management. They live in an environment that allows them at least to live socially as they might in the wild. To accommodate a growing gorilla population and new exhibit design, the Lincoln Park Zoo built the Lester E. Fisher Great Ape House in 1976. The exhibits were designed so that the gorillas could live in troops, as they would in the wild.

Gorillas are choosy about who they will mate with and so it has also been good fortune that the chemistry has worked and many babies have resulted.

In the management and care of the gorillas, there must be consistency. The same head keeper, Pat Sass, has been with them for more than twenty years. Mark Rosenthal, curator of mammals, has also been a constant at the zoo.

Lincoln Park Zoo has also been very successful in breeding other endangered species. The birth of Shanti, an Asian elephant, was a momentous occasion. Elephant births in zoos are very rare and each birth is critical. There are only 240 Asian elephants in North America (only 35,000 in the world). Over the past six years, there have been only ten successful births in zoos. Elephants, despite their size, have delicate health, and pregnancies last twenty-four months. With those odds, every precaution must be taken to assure a healthy pregnancy and birth. As with the western lowland gorilla,

The breeding program of lowland gorillas at the Lincoln Park Zoo has proven successful with examples like Otto, who fathered 15 children.

captive-born elephants are critical to the survival of an endangered species.

Bozie, Shanti's mother, came to Chicago in 1976 from an elephant orphanage when she was eighteen months old. Dr. Fisher, then the director, cared for her during the eighteen-hour flight from Sri Lanka. When she came of breeding age, a mate was found for her in Dickerson Park Zoo in Missouri. In a completely unconventional move, she was brought back home halfway through her two-year pregnancy. The Lincoln Park staff felt that she should be home, with people she knew best, for the important and possibly dangerous birth.

Birth was as new an experience for the zoo staff as it was for Bozie; no other elephant has ever been born there. In order to help the humans prepare for the experience, the staff spoke with each of the sixteen other zoos which have supervised an elephant birth.

They watched videos and prepared for every possible medical emergency and any other situation that might endanger mother or baby.

Bozie gave birth to Shanti without a hitch, surrounded by the humans who had cared for her over the years. People who were present at the birth say that Bozie pushed Shanti toward them after the delivery, but she quickly accepted the baby. She nuzzled the newborn to her feet and within a few hours the 270-pound Shanti was nursing contentedly. The first live birth of an Asian elephant at the Lincoln Park Zoo went flawlessly, perhaps in part because Bozie was in a place where she felt comfortable, with people she trusted.

Since its beginning with the donation of two pairs of trumpeter swans, the Lincoln Park Zoo has come a long way. Although it has remained a small municipal zoo, it has weathered more than a century of changing public attitudes about zoos.

Newborn Shanti, an Asian elephant, with her mother, Bozie. The birth of Shanti was a momentous occasion. Elephant births in zoos are very rare. There are only 240 Asian elephants in North America; over the past 6 years there have been only 10 successful births in zoos.

METROPOLITAN TORONTO ZOO
Toronto, Ontario, Canada
Opened 1974

In just over three hours, you can walk around the world at the Metropolitan Toronto Zoo in Ontario, Canada. By following the blue Round-the-World Trail, you will see mammals, birds, reptiles, amphibians, fish, invertebrates and plants that inhabit six regions of the world.

Metro Toronto Zoo is a "zoogeographic" zoo; the exhibits are organized around animals living in the same part of the world, unlike the Lincoln Park Zoo which is organized by species. The six zoogeographic regions represented over the 710 acres are Africa, Australasia, Eurasia, the Americas, the polar regions and Indo-Malaya.

The Australasia Pavilion, for example, exhibits plants, mammals and birds, as well as recreating a portion of a barrier reef. This exhibit of marine fish and invertebrates found in a reef community off the coast of Australia stresses the diversity of life in a world usually hidden.

Besides the trails—the blue Round-the-World Trail, the yellow Camel Trail to Eurasia and the purple Lion Trail to Indo-Malaya and Africa—there is the monorail, or trackless train, that provides an overview. Unlike some of the older zoos in North America, the Metro Toronto Zoo was created in the era of the modern zoological gardens.

All the animals are in exhibits that use today's technology to create realistic environments. All the utility lines are laid underground to minimize distraction from realistic scenes. In keeping with the environmental consciousness most zoos are trying to adopt, the Metro Toronto Zoo recycles, promotes nondisposable items in the restaurants, uses

Climate controlled and silent, this electrically powered train transports zoo visitors through 400 acres of the Rouge River Valley at the Metro Toronto Zoo.

recycled paper bedding for the animals and promotes environmental awareness in the schools.

Education is stressed throughout the zoo with "touch tables" (areas where people can hold and feel skins, foot items and other artifacts), demonstrations of animal behavior and keepers actively involved with the public. There is also an example here of the way zoos are working to save endangered species and reintroduce them to the wild on a global level.

The "Adopt a Pond" program sponsored by the zoo is an example of how many zoos move outside of their fences to guide people to work for the environment in their own communities. The Metro Toronto Zoo's Amphibian Interest Group, responding to the growing concern of scientists that amphibians are disappearing throughout the world, took action.

Reports have surfaced over the past decade that there do not seem to be as many frogs and toads as there once were, or should be. Perhaps this is because much of their habitat, wetlands and ponds, have been destroyed. In addition, amphibians are very sensitive to pesticides, chemicals and changes in the atmosphere. The conditions of the planet may be killing off the sensitive amphibians—with worrisome long-term implications for humans in a world where the balance of nature is out of kilter.

The aim of the "Adopt a Pond" program is to "...connect the loss of wetland habitat with the decline of amphibian populations. Empower students to act on behalf of frogs, toads, salamanders and newts and to introduce students to real-world problems where they can play an active role." With the help of zoo educators and teachers, interested students can adopt a local pond and protect existing habitat or restore damaged wetlands.

Metro Toronto Zoo hopes to involve more

Students working on "Adopt a Pond" program at the Metro Toronto Zoo.

than five thousand schools in Ontario.

Humans have often contributed unwittingly to the extinction of a species by introducing another animal into the habitat. For example, introduction of goats to the Galapagos Islands severely endangered the iguanas. The Galapagos hawk preys on the iguana from high in the air. The iguanas hid in the dense vegetation, but the goats ate their hiding places, leaving them easy targets for the hawks.

The saga of the Puerto Rican crested toad is interesting. For more than three decades, it was assumed to be extinct. The much bigger marine toad had been introduced to Puerto Rico from South America to control insects eating the sugar cane. Unfortunately, this toad ate the tiny four-inch crested toad and competed also for the same breeding ponds and food. Hurricanes and flooding had also taken their toll on the crested toads.

The Puerto Rican crested toad was thought to be extinct until as recently as 1990.

In 1990, a teacher was telling his pupils about how the toad had become extinct. A boy raised his hand to say, "No, it's not, I've seen them." The next day, he brought in living proof.

From there, the story becomes one of international cooperation, captive breeding in a zoo, understanding the value of protecting even such a small creature, the interest of the government and scientific trial and error.

A Metro Toronto Zoo biologist, Bob Johnson, became interested in saving the newfound toads from extinction. In his laboratory, he worked to uncover the secrets of getting the toads to breed, trying to duplicate the long dry season followed by torrential rains which the toads seem to need to get the temperature, humidity and timing of rain and drought just right. With so few animals in existence, there was very little room for error. Even when they laid and fertilized eggs, they

demanded a proper diet to grow into healthy toadlets. Johnson consulted with scientists from other zoos and the University of Puerto Rico.

By 1991, there were enough toads to put some back into the wild of Puerto Rico. The government of Puerto Rico, along with support from the Metro Toronto Zoo, educated the people of the region about the toad.

Biologists from Puerto Rico and Toronto followed the progress of the toads in the wild to learn more about them. It was nearly impossible to see them in the dense growth and the deep crevices between the rocks. So Johnson and his team wanted to track the toads with miniature radio transmitters. This device, the size of a pencil eraser, emits a signal that can be sent via satellite back to the researcher to track the animal.

After a great deal of trial and error, a Toronto sports-fashion designer came up with a tiny backpack that could carry a radio transmitter. With information from radio telemetry, a survival plan has been developed for the Puerto Rican crested toad. Additional "ponds" have been built for the toads. The zoo-breeding of Puerto Rican crested toads may no longer be necessary because the animals are doing so well back in their natural habitat, their natural place in the world.

Puerto Rican crested toad with backpack. The backpack holds a miniature radio transmitter which emits a signal that is sent via satellite back to researchers so that the toads can be tracked in their natural habitat.

THE NATIONAL ZOO'S CONSERVATION AND RESEARCH CENTER
FRONT ROYAL, VIRGINIA
Opened 1975

This facility is not open to the public. The Center, in the Shenandoah Valley, one and a half hours from Washington, D.C., is a part of the National Zoo and the Smithsonian Institution. The 3,150 acres of forest and fields are dedicated to protecting and breeding endangered species. It is a true conservation center.

The animals are not in exhibits. There are no popcorn stands, no camel rides and no visitors except scientists and invited guests. The focus is on saving species through zoological research, breeding and management, education and training.

When it became clearer, in their course of evolution, that zoos were going to have to step up the careful management of endangered species, the National Zoo began a search for land outside the boundaries of the city zoo and found it in Front Royal, Virginia, which had once been a remount station for the U.S. Cavalry where mounted soldiers could rest and change horses. There were already stables, barns and housing on the property as well as three thousand acres of fields, streams and cultivated land. The remote station is now one of the largest breeding centers in the United States for exotic animals, and it has gained an international reputation in zoological research and conservation biology.

The animals living in the Center are chosen to be there for one of several reasons: the wild population is severely threatened; there is a very small captive population; or it is a difficult species to breed in captivity, and in order to increase its chance of survival research must be done. Through these efforts, the Center has become a successful breeding facility for many animals, including Bactrian camels, zebras, golden lion tamarins, lesser pandas, Père David's deer, ten species of hoof stock and twenty-one species of bird.

Research is being done on reproduction, physiology and medical care of exotic animals. The solutions found here are used in zoos and help the animals still living in the wild.

View of the National Zoo's Conservation and Research Center, Front Royal, Virginia. What was once a remote station for the U.S. Cavalry is now a successful breeding facility for endangered species.

The National Zoo's Conservation and
Research Center at Front Royal,
Virginia, is a successful breeding
facility for endangered species. The
remote station is one of the largest
breeding centers in the United States
for exotic animals including; zebras,
Bactrian camels, golden lion
tamarins, lesser pandas and many
others. The Center has gained an
international reputation in zoological
research and conservation biology.

Another major focus at the Center is people —training conservationists to help preserve ecosystems.

Dr. Christen Wemmer, the associate director in charge of the Center, feels that in order for conservation to be successful, wilderness areas must be protected but, of equal importance, people need to understand the value of their country's wildlife. They need the information, the tools and the resources to manage what they have in their land.

It is important that there are trained conservationists working in their home countries to educate their own people about the value of the indigenous wildlife. (Zoo professionals feel it is their responsibility to share training and materials, especially in countries where money and other resources for protecting wildlife are limited.)

The Conservation and Research Center has become a three-thousand-acre classroom for trainees from around the world every summer for eight weeks; the Wildlife Conservation and Management Training Program draws park rangers, veterinarians, wildlife biologists and zookeepers from Thailand, Brazil, Malaysia, Central America and other parts of the world. They learn hands-on wildlife management from specialists, including Rasanayagam Rudran (Dr. Rudy, as his students call him), the Center's conservation program officer with a lifetime of experience studying wildlife behavior and ecology in Africa, Asia and South America. Dr. Rudran and his instructors pass along to his international students such things as the skill of radio-tracking animals and taking a census of plants or animals.

In the first five years, 199 wildlife biologists were trained from twenty-one countries. Dr. Rudran's work does not end after the summer. The rest of the year, he travels all over the world, giving his course wherever it is needed.

The land in Virginia provides the space to maintain threatened animals, the minds and materials to better understand their needs and the people to train others to influence tropical conservation through training and education.

There are too few of these facilities in the world at this time. But if zoos are truly going to become conservation centers in situ and ex situ, more facilities like the Conservation and Research Center must be created.

SISTER ZOOS
ZOO CONSERVATION OUTREACH GROUP

The Zoo Conservation Outreach Group (COG) was founded in 1988 by David Anderson, who was at the Audubon Park Zoo at the time, along with leaders of ten other North American zoos. They saw a need to assist zoos in South and Central America, who did not always have what they needed for the proper care of their animals, by facilitating exchanges of personnel, training, animals, consultation and financial support.

COG accomplished a great deal under the leadership of former executive director Sandra Skrei. She saw the dreadful condition of many zoos in Mesoamerica and recognized that meaningful contributions could be made with little effort.

Sometimes sending simple supplies like surgical thread, heaters or a microscope could make a large difference in how the sister zoo in South America could function. Sometimes the requirements were greater, including the need for funds for building renovations, training programs or transporting animals.

The COG has coordinated thirty-five North American zoos to work with sister zoos in Central America, arranging for such things as a veterinarian to do root canal surgery on a hippopotamus in the national zoo in El Salvador and a $250 contribution to the Belize Zoo for their education center, to facilitate staff exchanges and scholarships.

COG asks that when North American zoos build new exhibits, they raise ten percent extra to give directly to save rain forests. COG now has a membership program and travel opportunities which help sponsor conservation and education efforts in South and Central America.

Male golden lion tamarin in its native habitat, the Brazilian rain forest. There were once thousands living over millions of acres of Brazilian rain forests. It is estimated only a few hundred now exist in the wild.

WILDLIFE CONSERVATION SOCIETY
New York, New York
Established 1895

Since it was founded in 1895, The New York Zoological Society, today's Wildlife Conservation Society, has been a front-runner in the evolution of zoos throughout North America and the world. The Society continues today as a leader in exhibit design, animal care, research and development of a visionary path for zoos to follow into the future.

The mission of the Wildlife Conservation Society has always been conservation, education and research. The Wildlife Conservation Society has become an umbrella sheltering four zoos, a conservation and research center, an aquarium and the work of field biologists in all parts of the world.

The name change reflects what it does and the path it believes zoos will be taking in the coming decades. The Wildlife Conservation Society announced the name change not only of the Society but of its branches as well. The Bronx Zoo is now called Bronx Zoo/Wildlife Conservation Park, the Central Park Zoo is now the Central Park Wildlife Center, the zoos in the boroughs of Queens and Brooklyn are also named wildlife centers, and the aquarium is now the Aquarium for Wildlife Conservation. Of great importance to all the work of wildlife conservation is the Wildlife Conservation Society's international programs. The Wildlife Conservation Society field programs are currently 225 strong in 46 countries. The Society also has a branch on St. Catherine's Island, St. Catherine's Wildlife Conservation Center, off the coast of Georgia, dedicated exclusively to the care and breeding of endangered animals.

In 1887, Theodore Roosevelt, who was a big-game hunter, and several other men concerned about the overwhelming destruction of wildlife in America founded the Boone and Crockett Club. The slaughter of animals was occurring as people moved into the frontiers of America where the quantities of wildlife seemed endless. Birds, wolves and bison were being killed at an overwhelming rate. In fact, of the ten million bison that once ranged across the plains of America, just over a few dozen remained by 1901. Because of the Wildlife Conservation Society's intervention, the remaining bison were captured and protected while their numbers increased, and then, years later, they were released back into the plains where today there is again a strong population.

From the outset, the Wildlife Conservation Society and its institutions were born from a desire to preserve wildlife, to study it and to bring to all people an understanding of the value of animals and ecosystems. Wildlife conservation and the understanding of wildlife in situ has always been a major emphasis for the Society.

The Society's first project, the design and construction of what was then called The New York Zoological Park, began to take shape in 1895. A member of the Society, Madison Grant, made it clear that his mission was to have a world-class zoo in New York, bigger than the zoos of Europe. The Society began the search for land, believing that they needed about three hundred acres. That was twice the acreage of the National Zoo in Washington, D.C., and five times that of the Berlin Zoo in Germany.

The city transferred to the Society land near the newly formed Botanical Garden. Money was raised, and William Hornaday, the founder of the National Zoo, was hired as the first director of the Bronx Zoo, which opened on November 8, 1899. From opening day, it was a huge success. A reputation for excellent animal management and creative exhibits was quickly established.

In 1902, the Society was asked to take over the New York Aquarium and manage it on a scientific and educational basis, as they had done so successfully with the Bronx Zoo.

In addition to the keepers and management of the Bronx Zoo, most of the professional staff were scientists researching the natural behavior of the animals, in the zoo and in the wild. This idea of actually observing animals in their natural habitat was advanced thinking for the day. Indeed, the work of the Wildlife Conservation Society was really begun as what would become the largest field conservation program sponsored by a zoo.

Since its beginnings, the Society has sponsored wildlife research in the field. Even two years before the Bronx Zoo opened, the Society sent researchers to Alaska to report back on the destruction taking place and what the Society could do to help protect the environment. Since then, there have been more than one thousand field studies sponsored by the Wildlife Conservation Society.

The Society launched a magazine in 1907, *Zoologica*, as a place for its scientific papers to be published. Describing the scientific staff of the zoo and aquarium, the magazine said that they were not the sort to be interested in the "lifeless cabinet" or museum. Rather, they "...sought a new and inspiring field which had been relatively little pursued, namely the observation of the living bird and the living mammal, wherever

possible in its own environment."

The Wildlife Conservation Society's research has involved the study not just of animals but of the entire ecosystem, to find solutions to the problems created by human overpopulation. If the needs of the people are not addressed, they cannot be expected to place the welfare of elephants over the needs of their children. Farmers do not wish to see their land taken and given to a national park to protect wildlife. They shoot as pests monkeys that raid their crops, and if their families are hungry they will shoot bushmeat as they have for generations. For decades, the Wildlife Conservation Society has been working to understand the ecosystem well enough to find workable solutions for cohabitation of wildlife and humans.

As long ago as 1959, the Society's Wildlife Protection Fund sent $150,000 to Tanzania and Uganda in Africa to fund work toward improving life for the people and the wildlife. The funds were used to drill wells and water holes so that the Masai, the people who live

Of the 10 million bison that once ranged across the plains of America just a few dozen remained by 1901. Because of the Society's early intervention there continues today to be a strong wild population.

1907—bison shipping from the Bronx Zoo to the Wichita, Kansas, Zoo as part of the captive breeding program for reintroduction into the wild. William Hornaday is at left.

on the land and depend on their cattle to provide food and money, would not have to go into the park to get the water they needed. The Society also trained native wardens to fly light airplanes to control poaching and to monitor the migration of herds of wildebeests and other animals—so they were able to earn income by protecting their country's wildlife.

In its conservation parks, the Wildlife Conservation Society has always tried to educate people about the interrelationships of all living things. Adhering to the concept of barless cages introduced early in the century by Carl Hagenbeck, a German zoo director, the African Plains opened to the public in the spring of 1941. The first Sunday, 84,727 people came to see it.

Since then, many innovative exhibits have been built by the Bronx Zoo: the Penguin House (1947), with a glass-faced pool, where the zoo visitor first had the oppor-tunity to see how penguins "fly" underwater; the World of Darkness (1959), where the visitor could observe the nocturnal world; the World of Birds (1972), where only light keeps birds and humans apart; and the magnificent JungleWorld (1989), where the most up-to-date technology, some invented by the zoo, allows the visitor to experience a rain forest.

Certainly, when the Wildlife Conservation Society was created almost one hundred years ago, it would have been hard to imagine the strength and effect it would have on the future world of animal conservation, education and research.

Indian elephants in Wild Asia exhibit.

Siberian tiger in Wild Asia exhibit.

Chapter Two

A BRIEF WORLD HISTORY OF ZOOS

Red ants, rhinoceros, slime molds, blue whales and humans all have evolved over millions of years to fill their special niches on the planet. People domesticated some animals, feared and avoided others and bestowed on some the qualities of gods.

As clever as the human animal is, only in the past three thousand years have we had the capability to capture and confine large animals. Now we can do this with ease, using very sophisticated techniques.

The story of zoos has been reconstructed by scholars of history, anthropology, philosophy and architecture. Evidence has revealed that all the great civilizations kept animals on display, usually in the centers of wealth, the cities.

Originally, collecting animals was the privilege of kings and other potentates who wanted exotic animals as treasures for their personal enjoyment. Such royalty kept animals as signs of their power and wealth. They were the ones who organized, owned and saw the collections—not the common man. Royalty bestowed exotic animals as gifts, like gold and jewels. "Collections" were random groupings of animals. Over the ages, they became more organized but with little thought or understanding of what the animals needed. The animals were confined in cages designed not for comfort but so the visitors could get a good view.

EARLIEST COLLECTIONS

A stone tablet dated 2300 B.C. described a collection of rare animals in the Sumerian city of Ur.

Around 1500 B.C., Egyptian pharaoh Thutmose III is reported to have kept a collection of animals for his pleasure. His stepmother, Queen Hatshepsut, is recorded as having sent expeditions in search of wildlife. At great expense, she sent out five ships to find then-unknown animals and was rewarded with many species, including monkeys, cheetahs and giraffes, captured for her collection.

In 1100 B.C., Assyrian king Tiglath-pileser

had large preserves for wild animals.

Emperor Wen Wang of the earliest Chinese dynasty (Zhou Dynasty, 1027–221 B.C.) called the park where he kept animals the "Garden of Intelligence." It was a place to study and learn from the marvels of nature and wildlife.

These early collections were signs of greatness. Rulers felt more powerful and wealthy surrounded by unusual and dangerous animals. Collecting also gave humans the opportunity to study animals in order to understand nature better and to see if there were unknown animals that could be domesticated or in any way used to benefit human beings.

As man explored the distant continents, he discovered a great variety of animals. These "new and strange" species became treasures like the spices, gold and jewels brought back by early explorers.

In Roman times (27 B.C.–476 A.D.), the display of animals for aggrandizement and entertainment reached its peak. Roman leaders were able to demonstrate their power through the power of wild animals. In the col-

iseums, like today's football stadiums, huge numbers of animals such as bears and lions died in fights with each other or against gladiators; unarmed people were thrown to the lions as punishment. Many of the animals were captured from the wild, but some were also bred in captivity so there would always be a supply for these bloody spectacles.

Roman poet and scholar Marcus Terentius Varro (116–27 B.C.) allowed his guests to dine in his aviary after they picked which of the beautiful birds they wished to eat.

Roman emperor Nero (37–68 A.D.) had a pet tigress named Phoebe, which often joined him for dinner; if someone there displeased the emperor, the offender might become a special treat for Phoebe's dinner.

Not all individuals used their collections with disregard for the animals' welfare. Alexander the Great, leader of Macedonia (336–323 B.C.), who conquered and ruled most of what was then the known world, including Persia, India and Egypt, kept elephants, bears, monkeys and a great variety of

In the coliseum, huge numbers of animals such as bears and lions died in fights with each other or against gladiators.

animals his men brought to him from the conquests of his armies. Despite his awesome power, he is said nonetheless to have been gentle and careful with his vast collection. When Alexander the Great left his collection to King Ptolemy I of Egypt, Ptolemy established what is known to be the first organized zoo. Aristotle (384–322 B.C.), one of the great Greek philosophers and Alexander's tutor, observed the animals in the leader's collection and may have been one of the first people to study the behavior of animals just out of curiosity. From his observations, Aristotle wrote an encyclopedia of zoology called *History of Animals*, describing three hundred species of vertebrates.

Following this culturally rich period of history, the Middle Ages (after the fall of the Roman Empire in the fifth century) was a time of growth for cities, caused by increased trade and the rise of the Church. Scant attention was paid to the arts, education or nature. It seems that collections of animals had little importance during this time.

By the thirteenth century, animal collections were again in vogue; anybody who was anybody wanted one. Kings and emperors exchanged gifts of animals. Frederick II, king of Sicily and emperor of the Holy Roman Empire (1215–1250), considered a great patron of the arts and sciences, kept many animals in his collection, including hyenas and a giraffe. Three of his cities had animal collections, many for scientific study.

Frederick traded his giraffe to the sultan of Egypt for a polar bear. It is hard to imagine how a polar bear ever survived a trip to Egypt in the twelfth century—a voyage of thousands of miles in the hold of a small wooden sailing ship. Frederick also trained cheetahs, extraordinarily fast animals native to Africa, for the hunt, rather than using dogs. No game animal could outrun the cheetah.

Frederick apparently liked his animals enough to travel with them wherever he went. Even on a voyage to Worms, Germany, to be married, he brought along elephants, camels, lions, monkeys and cheetahs. His

A representation of wagons and boats, which in the form of a convoy, carry the beasts and provisions necessary for the sustenance of those that would attend the special events of kings.

wedding was, of course, an important occasion, so the animals were dressed in gems, ornaments and beautiful cloth.

Until the eighteenth century, animals on display were to be seen only by other important people. But, as the nobility lost power and control over the common people in different parts of the world, animal collections became more accessible to all. Captive collections on display came to be called "menageries," defined simply as being collections of wild animals kept in cages. (Although 1712 was the first time the word "menagerie" was used in print, it is used here in the broader sense to describe more organized collections.)

MENAGERIES

In menageries, the animals were still looked at as mere curiosities. The cages were built with no sense of what the animals might need for a healthy life, but rather just so that spectators could get a good, close look. There was no place for the animals to hide from view. A bare box made with metal bars, or a pit in the ground, seemed, to the builders of menageries, the best solution.

Henry I (1068–1135), the fourth son of William the Conqueror, had a great collection of animals. His grandson, Henry III, continued the tradition when he became king of England (1216–1272) and transferred the royal residence to the Tower of London. He built what we now refer to as the "Royal Menagerie," a group of special cages displayed outside the Tower for other royalty to see.

In 1254, he built a special house for an elephant he received as a gift from Louis IX of France. The elephant was apparently the first to travel to England. In keeping with the small, dark cages of the menagerie, the elephant house was just big enough for the elephant to fit into.

Animals kept in the English menageries were sometimes also used, as by the Romans, for more aggressive entertainment. Tigers fought lions, and bears fought dogs, for the amusement of royal guests.

During this time, the common people had few privileges. The royalty was in full control. Although the people of London were not allowed to visit the Royal Menagerie, they were ordered to pay a tax for care of the

Cheetahs were often used in India to hunt other game such as antelopes.

animals. According to a story from that time, when sufficient food couldn't be produced for the big polar bear, the keeper took the bear to the Thames River and let him fish for his own food.

When Henry VI married Margaret of Anjou in 1445, she was given a lion as a wedding gift. She was so pleased that she expanded the menagerie at the Tower, bringing in many more animals. The Royal Menagerie prospered for several more generations.

In Florence, Italy, during the late 1400s, there was a large and famous menagerie. During this period of the Renaissance, animals were viewed as creatures of beauty and nobility. Images of lions and wolves appeared on family emblems. The animals in the menagerie were used as models for paintings, and they appear in many of the extraordinary works of art of the time. Leonardo da Vinci, the great artist and scientific genius, kept animals of his own as models.

During the fifteenth century, Germany and Austria also had menageries. The one in Marienburg kept marine mammals—seals and a walrus. This collection also had several aurochs, a wild ox now extinct.

One of the best menageries was established by Akbar (1542–1605), the third Mogul emperor of India. At his death, he had five thousand elephants and one thousand camels. He forbade animal fights and admired the animals under his protection. His collection was open to his subjects.

Akbar may have been an exception in his appreciation of wild animals. Other powerful rulers were not so kind. An example of the need to conquer all life, rather than appreciate it, comes from the "New World." Across the Atlantic, exploration of this new world, the Americas, led to the discovery of animals never before seen by Europeans.

In 1521, the Spaniard Cortez made his way to Central America and Mexico, a land populated by Aztecs. When he reached their capital, Tenochtitlán, he and his soldiers found a magnificent city. The entry into the town was lined with beautiful aviaries of singing birds. The Aztec leader, Montezuma, kept a spectacular collection of animals in cages throughout the city: jaguars and pumas in pens with bronze bars, fish in deep copper bowls, armadillos, monkeys and reptiles in cages. The animals were well cared for. But Cortez was not there to learn, he was there to conquer. The city, the people and the animals were destroyed.

On the European continent, especially in Russia, Poland and Sweden, the animal most commonly kept as a show of power was the bear. Ivan the Terrible (1530–1584) kept bears in dens within his castle. This made it very easy to dispose of any of his enemies who got too close. For generations, the kings of France built and stocked

Left: Akbar the Great and his menagerie of exotic animals.

Bottom: Cortez and Montezuma.

menageries. King Louis XIV, who reigned from 1643 to 1715, had menageries at all his châteaux. Animal cages were scattered around the royal property. But at Versailles, Louis XIV changed the concept of the menagerie. He designed it so that all the animal enclosures were grouped in one area and were painted with scenes of flowers and birds.

In Vienna, Austria, Holy Roman Emperor Francis I gave his wife Maria Theresa a collection of animals as a gift in 1752. This was named the Schonbrunn Zoo (or Menagerie). It is said that Maria Theresa liked to have her meals among the elephants, camels and zebras.

By the 1790s, change was coming. The people were taking power away from royalty. Among the things they claimed for themselves was the right to see the private collections of captive animals. During the French Revolution, people stormed the menagerie at Versailles, the summer home of Marie Antoinette. The smaller animals were released, some eaten by the looters while others escaped into the nearby forests. Apparently the people thought better of opening the doors to the rhinos, lions and other large animals and left them there in the care of their keeper, who had loyally stayed to protect them.

The private lives of nobility and kings were breaking down; lands and treasures were redistributed. Eventually many menageries were collected to become one. This menagerie from Versailles was taken to the Jardin des Plantes, a botanical garden in Paris.

In 1793, the royal animals that had remained in Versailles were also sent to the Jardin des Plantes. It was decided that they should be a collection of scientific value, to be studied as wonders of nature. The idea of the zoological garden had arrived.

Across the English Channel, the common citizens of London had been allowed to visit the animals in the Royal Menagerie at the Tower of London since the early 1700s. They had to pay a few pence admission, or they could contribute a dog or cat as a meal for one of the big cats or bears.

The next century was a time of discovery and expansion for the British. The Victorian period in England (mid-1800s to 1900) brought with it a new curiosity about natural history and science, including zoology (the branch of biological sciences specializing in the study of animals, including anatomy, evolution and behavior).

ZOOLOGICAL GARDENS

In the early nineteenth century, the development of large cities and increasing wealth led to the preservation of natural areas and the design of parkland for recreation. The survival of a natural world became an increasing concern, and a hunger for a scientific understanding of wildlife developed. Plants and animals were protected and exhibited together in parks. The root of the word "zoo" comes from the ancient Greek word "zoion," meaning "living being." From that came "zoology," the study of living beings, animals. So came the evolution and naming of the zoological park or garden.

The period's strong interest in natural history and animals created an environment in which the Zoological Society of

Swedish botanist Carolus Linnaeus (1707–1778) was the first to establish principles for naming and classifying plants and animals, to bring systematic order to the great array of living things. Many zoos display animals according to the way they were first categorized by Linnaeus.

London could be established.

It was also during the Victorian period that Charles Darwin (1809–1882), the famous British naturalist, sailed on the ship HMS *Beagle*. The *Beagle* stopped at the remote Galapagos Islands in the Pacific Ocean, where Darwin observed that the animals, although similar to those in Europe, had evolved quite differently.

From his notes of that five-year journey, he wrote a book called *The Origin of Species by Means of Natural Selection*. "Darwinism" is his theory of evolution that still stands today.

He observed that: In any animal population there are individual variations, and more off-spring of any species are born than are needed to keep the species alive. Darwin concluded that the survivors are those best suited to survive disease, natural disasters, changing environment and competition for food and shelter. This natural way of selecting which ones outlive the others is called "survival of the fittest." The "fittest" animals are able to breed and pass on these advantageous survival characteristics to their offspring.

A zoological society is interested in establishing a planned zoological garden in which to keep zoo animals on view to the public. These interested citizens and scholars raise money to acquire the land and construct buildings and cages, gather the animals and hire staff.

It was with the help of the Zoological Society of London that the zoological garden in Regent's Park, London, opened in 1828. The stated purpose of the Regent's Park Zoo was to study captive animals in order to better understand their wild relatives. The British wanted to understand the wildlife they discovered as their colonies expanded to new parts of the world. Museums of natural history, botanical gardens and zoological gardens became important to the culture.

The Regent's Park Zoo became an example for the zoological gardens that would be established across the United Kingdom, Europe and the United States during the next stage of zoo evolution.

During the 1800s, in cities throughout Europe and England, zoological gardens exploded in popularity. For the city dweller, they provided places of greenery that were a relief from the ugly, dirty cities of this period.

Zoological gardens became such a part of the culture that songs were written about them. It is perhaps because of an English song, "Walking in the Zoo Is an Okay Thing to Do," that the abbreviation "zoo" came to be used. *The Oxford English Dictionary* gives 1847 as the date the word "zoo" was first used in print.

Collections, menageries, zoological gardens—all displays of animals in captivity—have evolved and reflected current culture over thousands of years, in all parts of the world. Today zoological parks continue to evolve in order to meet the critical needs of a planet in trouble. They are evolving to become what leaders in the field call "conservation centers."

Because American history, compared to global history, is brief, we can clearly see the process of zoo evolution taking place in the United States.

Chapter Three
TRAVELING SHOWS
TO IMMERSION EXHIBITS

I n the late 1700s, as the Eastern Seaboard was being settled, most of the continent that stretched to the west was, as far as the early colonists were concerned, wild and unexplored. People were eager to get a glimpse of the wildlife they might encounter on their voyage west. Traveling shows selling miracle medicines and other useful and useless objects passed through the growing towns. Taking advantage of the people's curiosity, they carried caged animals as part of the show. People paid to see them. Circuses and menageries toured the country, stopping even in towns with populations of fewer than five thousand people. These traveling menageries were common in Europe, and the idea quickly spread in the United States. For the local tavern, a caged bear or eagle was a sure way to attract customers.

New American cities like New York, Philadelphia and Boston were now substantial settlements. People turned their attention from survival to the enjoyment of the wonders and wealth of this new world. Concert halls, theaters and museums were built. "Curiosities," including fossils, minerals, plants and stuffed animals, were put on exhibit in what were called "cabinets" or museums of natural history.

Early in American history, circuses and menageries had many similarities. Both were collections of caged animals touring the country for the amusement of the people. Menageries took root in growing communities. They no longer had to travel to find customers. It was not necessary to import all the animals from across the oceans: the wildlife found on the North American continent was exotic enough.

By the early eighteenth century, three developments had made it possible for menageries to become a real part of North American life: the growth of the cities provided an eager, stable audience; travel to Europe, Africa, South America and the Orient was less hazardous and more common; transporting the animals, "bringing them back alive," was successful more of the time.

Travel to other continents, especially Africa, to hunt big game became a fabulous adventure for young North Americans, who might return with trophies for the wall, stuffed specimens for a museum or live animals to sell to a menagerie, circus or private collection. Additionally, museum curators and scholars of natural science sent out collecting expeditions in North America and around the world.

One famous adventurer and hunter was Teddy Roosevelt, the twenty-sixth president of the United States. He set out to collect as many rare animals as possible. Some were sold to menageries or circuses. Many, stuffed, ended up in natural history museums. Both his sons, Teddy, Jr., and Kermit, were also hunters. They are recognized for being the first foreigners to shoot giant pandas in China.

Capturing wild animals was often a very dangerous occupation. Yet, there were plenty of people who loved the adventure—and the money.

Especially for the animals, capture and travel was torturous. Most died from poor diet, stress and, in the case of thousands of babies, loneliness. Through years of trial and error and luck, expeditions did arrive with enough live animals to make the trips worthwhile. Animals that survived the trip were put in cages where they would remain for the rest of their lives, long or short. Those that died in the menageries were easily replaced. The supply in the wild seemed endless. The public was curious, scientists were interested and the explorers and traders could make money.

Menageries consisted of rows of caged animals: one species alone in a cage next to a lone individual of a different species—like a stamp collection. And indeed, the nickname for these menageries is "postage stamp collection."

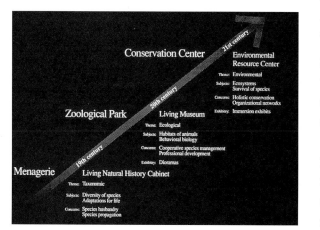

Top: Dr. Rabb's zoo evolutionary chart from menageries to contemporary conservation centers.

Left: Early 1800s illustration depicting animal menagerie at the Central Park Zoo.

From 1861 to 1865, the Civil War took the energy and attention of the country. In the years following the war, American cities really grew in size and strength, and with them grew menageries.

New York City was one of the few big cities in the United States before the Civil War. As early as 1781, menageries were in New York City. A privately owned menagerie described in 1789 had a tiger, orangutan, sloth, baboon, buffalo, crocodile, lizards and snakes.

Since 1861, there has been a collection of animals at Fifth Avenue and Sixty-fourth Street in Central Park, the same location that today is the Central Park Wildlife Center. At first, like the menageries before it, it was just a jumble of donated animals on display: a black

bear, a pair of kerry cows, Virginia deer, monkeys, raccoons, foxes, opossums, ducks, swans, eagles, pelicans and parrots. It was a place to leave unwanted animals from private collections and carnivals. Some of the animals were kept in the basement of the Arsenal, a building which still stands today as headquarters for the Wildlife Conservation Society and the New York City Parks Department. Other animals lived in buildings on the land around the Arsenal.

In its first fifty years, the Central Park Zoo was definitely a menagerie, a group of small, barred cages. By today's standards it was awful. Over the past decade, it has evolved into a jewel of a small urban zoological park and is now known as the Central Park Wildlife Center.

But in the late 1800s, as a menagerie, it was a center of entertainment both for the wealthy Fifth Avenue strollers and for the poor who were looking for a break from their daily working lives. Newly arrived immigrants lived in dark, crowded tenements on the Lower East Side of New York. A trip up to the green of Central Park to see the menagerie was well worth the walk or the nickel fare on the trolley.

In 1868, the Central Park menagerie sent two pairs of swans to Lincoln Park in Chicago for their pond. The swans were the beginning of what was to become the Lincoln Park Zoo.

Gifts of other animals followed, and by 1873 Lincoln Park had twenty-seven mammals and forty-eight birds. These were the first two American menageries that evolved into respected zoological gardens.

Both of these menageries located in city parks were managed by the parks departments. The employees reported to the parks commissioners, who might not know anything about the care of animals. One month the employees would be raking leaves; the next they might be feeding the animals.

It was not until 1980 that the Wildlife Conservation Society signed an agreement with the city to take over the management of the Central Park Zoo and the other zoos

1886—people strolling through the Central Park Zoo. The tall building in the background is the Arsenal, which still stands today.

operated by the Parks Department in the boroughs of Brooklyn and Queens. These zoos, although owned by the city, are now managed by the the Wildlife Conservation Society. Today, the facility for exotic animals that still occupies the same spot in Central Park, with the same landmark buildings, has been transformed from a menagerie into a state-of-the-art wildlife conservation center for the twenty-first century.

By the mid-1850s, Philadelphia was the center of political and cultural American life. Some politicians, scientists and businessmen thought that a zoo would be a great addition to the city. Several of these gentlemen had seen the London Zoo and had come away impressed by how a zoological garden can benefit a city.

In 1859, Philadelphia, the largest American city, was already home to the first American botanical garden, the Bartram Botanical Garden; the Peale Museum, a fine natural history museum; and European-style public parks, gardens, theaters, concert halls and circuses.

On March 21, 1859, leaders of the city created the Zoological Society of Philadelphia. It was the idea of a Dr. William Camac, who had traveled through Europe and had seen the zoological gardens. It was his thought that a zoological garden for Philadelphia would be another cultural first for the growing city.

It would still be more than fifteen years until land was secured, buildings erected and animals installed. Not everyone had agreed with Dr. Camac that a zoo should be a high

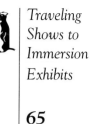
1889—visitors at the sea lion pool, Lincoln Park Zoo.

priority. Progress was stopped by the Civil War. But Dr. Camac's attention did not waver, and in 1872 he called the Zoological Society together again.

Unlike the early menageries, the Philadelphia Zoological Park was planned for. Animals were collected with a purpose, permanent structures were built to house the animals and a professional full-time staff was hired.

During the next two years, the Zoological Society chose a location and hired an architect to draw plans for a zoological garden and to build the enclosures and buildings that would house the animals. An animal collector, Frank J. Thompson, was sent off to collect animals for the first American zoological park. To raise additional funds, the society offered memberships to the zoo.

On a clear July 1, 1874, the gates opened to three thousand visitors. Adults paid twenty-five cents, children ten cents. When they saw the wonderful monkey house, bird house, prairie dog village —the only one in the world—sea lion pools and exotic animals from Australia and the Pacific Islands, there were few complaints.

Twenty-six years later, in keeping with zoos as places of study, the Philadelphia Zoo again set a trend, opening the first research laboratory associated with a zoo.

Following the Revolutionary War, Washington, D.C., had become the nation's capital. It had a world-renowned natural history museum, the Smithsonian Institution, and, as of 1870, a zoological society. Yet it did not have a zoological garden until 1889. The Zoological Society was unable to gather enough support. A menagerie was created as part of the Smithsonian collection of living animals for the taxidermists (people who stuff and mount animals for display). The

Above:
Dr. William Camac.

Right:
William Hornaday, chief taxidermist at the Smithsonian's U.S. National Museum, leads an endangered bison calf on the Mall, near the Smithsonian Castle, in 1886. Hornaday was instrumental in persuading both Houses of Congress to pass legislation in 1889 establishing the National Zoological Park in Washington, D.C. He is considered the guiding spirit behind the creation of the National Zoo.

taxidermists were to use the menagerie animals as models for those they were preserving for the museum.

A taxidermist, William T. Hornaday, was put in charge of the small living collection he brought to the museum. The animals were put in a simple building near the Smithsonian. On the last day of December 1887, the public was admitted. For a time there was an "exhibit" of domestic dogs in the menagerie. The barking distracted everyone and the dogs were soon given away.

The collection grew until there was pressure on the Congress of the United States to provide funds to open a "Zoological Park in the District of Columbia for the advancement of science and the instruction and recreation of the people."

A beautiful area of 175 acres within the city's Rock Creek Valley was selected in 1889

for the zoological garden, which was opened in 1891 to study animals as well as exhibit them.

In 1895, not long after the opening of the zoological garden in the nation's capital, the New York Zoological Society, now called the Wildlife Conservation Society, was formed for the purpose of "encouraging and advancing the study of zoology…furnishing instruction and recreation to the people."

In a report that would be important for the future of the Society and the evolution of all zoos, it was stated that the Society would promote "cooperation with other organizations in the preservation of the native animals of North America and encouragement of the growing sentiment against their wanton destruction."

The Wildlife Conservation Society went to work to gather support and money for the

19th-century photograph of visitors at the National Zoological Park relaxing at Rock Creek.

building of a zoological garden outside of the city. Four years later, on November 8, 1899, with William T. Hornaday as director (he quit his work with the Smithsonian), the Bronx Zoo opened.

America was becoming a wealthy country. As cities grew, the public valued natural resources, including zoological parks. Zoos were becoming centers for recreation. Twenty-three were established in the United States by the early 1900s, including the National Zoo, the Bronx Zoo, the San Diego Zoo and Zoo Atlanta. No major park system was considered complete without a zoological or botanical garden.

Still, we had much to learn about the care of captive animals. Animal management, largely by trial and error, was not adequate by today's standards. Few people had ever seen these animals in their natural habitats. The trappers and hunters did not bother to study animal behavior. There was little information about what the animals needed to eat or how they lived in the wild. For the keepers responsible for the captive animals, it was mostly guesswork.

The visitors to the early zoological gardens saw many different animals. However, they did not learn much significant information about the animals. Perhaps there was a sign saying "lion," but there was no description of where it came from, how old it was, how it behaved in nature or anything else about it, except maybe its feeding time.

To keep the visitors returning again and again (and paying again and again), the animal collection had to remain interesting. For a long time, which is only now fading, the zoological gardens were in fierce competition with one another. If one zoo got a giraffe, the next zoo wanted to get a giraffe and a rhinoceros. When a "cute," unusual animal like a koala or giant panda arrived, it was certain to attract many visitors. Soon zoos were compet-

Baby African elephant being shipped to the Bronx Zoo.

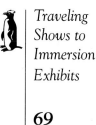
ing to show the most intriguing specimens. New animals kept on coming, animals that no other collection could boast of having.

The North American zoogoer was well entertained but learned little significant information. Animal shows were common: dancing bears, elephant parades and dressed chimpanzees. A description from a zoo guidebook gives a good example: "In the summer of 1911, the daily open-air exhibition of nine apes dining at 4 o'clock…in the large outside cage at the Primate House will long be remembered by the crowds of visitors who saw it." The guidebook goes on to state that such shows were meant to illustrate how "human like" chimpanzees are.

In early zoological gardens, more often than not animals were kept caged alone, even animals that we now know live in social groups or families, like chimpanzees and gorillas. With many animals to care for and little time or money, keepers had to make care of the animals as simple as possible. The early cages often looked like bathrooms, made completely of tile and concrete that was easy to hose down. Such cleanliness was considered crucial to keeping the animals healthy, and it made life easier for the keepers, no matter how unnatural such cages were for the animals. This manner of keeping the animals gave rise to the term "the toilet era."

A zoo animal was kept in a bare cage with heavy iron bars separating it from the visitor. The animal had nowhere to hide, often no place to get up off the floor. There were no objects, or "furniture," in the cage. The big cats, lions or tigers, might have shelves to sleep on. It was a monotonous way to live, with absolutely nothing to interrupt the boredom except one or two meals a day and being moved around when the cage was cleaned.

By the early 1900s, even greater care had to be taken to make sure the animals would not sicken and die—not only for humane reasons.

Baby elephant's arrival at the Bronx Zoo.

Elephant House at the Bronx Zoo, early 1900s. Many different types of animals were displayed at the Elephant House.

Getting animals from the wild was becoming very difficult. The seemingly endless supply of animals had dried up. Many animals had been hunted and trapped to extinction, or near extinction. Also, foreign governments realized that the animals living in their countries had value as natural resources; if they were removed, the country should be paid. Yet, even with increased difficulties in capture and export, it would still be many decades before capture in the wild slowed significantly. And it still has not stopped.

The limits on capture meant that zoological gardens had to become much more careful with their residents. They had to learn to keep them in the best of health and, rather than depend on getting new animals, learn to breed them in the zoo. In addition, animal babies attracted the human crowds.

Slowly, it was becoming obvious that, to remain healthy and breeding, zoo animals needed surroundings that were more like their natural environments.

In order to follow the evolution of the zoo, we have to go back to Europe for a moment. In 1907, a German named Carl Hagenbeck opened his own zoo. The ideas and philosophy demonstrated in his zoo would change animal exhibits around the world.

Hagenbeck began his career as a collector of wild animals for zoos and circuses, then he trained animals for circus acts. Always looking for a new hook, he expanded on the exotic animal show by bringing together people of different world cultures and putting them on display in environments that resembled their native lands. Hagenbeck's shows touring through Europe included Laplanders with reindeer and Inuits with polar bears. In Berlin, on a single day in 1878, sixty-two thousand people visited the Hagenbeck traveling exhibit on display at that city's zoo. Yet he was not satisfied. He was always looking for new ways to display animals. In his extensive travels around the world, he had studied animal behavior in order to train them for his acts, and he wanted something more.

Carl Hagenbeck decided to open his own zoo. It would not be an ordinary zoo, with animals in cage after cage. Rather, he wrote, "I wished to exhibit them not as captives, confined to narrow spaces and looked at between

Bear dens at the
Bronx Zoo, early
1900s.

bars, but as free to wander from place to place within as large limits as possible and with no bars to obstruct the view and serve as a reminder of captivity."

He designed a zoo in which the animals had maximum freedom and the human visitors could feel they were seeing the animals nearly in the wild. He began to build the Hagenbeck Tierpark in 1890. It is still there, owned and operated by the Hagenbeck family.

Hagenbeck introduced a new concept of building moats around the exhibits. He used his experience as an animal trainer to test how high and far the animals could jump. The moats were not obvious to the visitors. They were camouflaged with plants and landscaping. But for the animals, these deep moats were intimidating obstacles not to be jumped over, into or out of.

Hagenbeck was able to design the exhibits to look as if predator and prey, lion and zebra, were in the same exhibit. In reality, a concealed moat was keeping them apart. Now the visitors could see a lion sprawled out on a big rock, surrounded by several lionesses and cubs tumbling in the grass. The panorama would include a herd of zebras, antelope and a few ostriches in a field just behind the lions. A whole picture of natural life came alive. The public could see the interrelationship of animals, begin to picture what the African landscape looked like and learn about predators, prey and habitats.

People began to appreciate the animals in a new light, seeing them no longer in cages behind thick iron bars, but rather in more naturalistic exhibits where there was at least an illusion of freedom. There was more to do and see for the animals as well. It was a major step in changing the public idea of how animals could and should be kept in captivity.

Some zoo directors, including William Hornaday at the Bronx Zoo, challenged this new idea of naturalistic exhibits, saying the animals would be too far away from the visitors. But most embraced the idea and rushed to change their exhibits. Hagenbeck's sons went to Detroit, Michigan, to design that city's new zoo. They also contributed to the design of the Cincinnati Zoo. The Brookfield Zoo in Chicago sent a delegation to Hamburg, Germany, to study with the Hagenbecks and

African Plains exhibit at the Bronx Zoo, inspired by Carl Hagenbeck's theories of naturalistic exhibit design.

incorporated many of the ideas into the Brookfield Zoo. Many other North American zoos quickly followed with naturalistic exhibits.

Hagenbeck had introduced more than a new way of displaying animals; he improved life for the animals. This trend continues to grow today. And today what we learn in the zoo can also be used in the wild.

In the 1930s, following the Depression, the Public Works Program created by President Franklin Roosevelt put many people to work. This was a tremendous help to zoos, giving them the manpower for badly needed modernization and repair. Then, once again, a war, World War II, interrupted the development of zoos. It was not until the 1950s that they again flourished. The 1960s were a time of great change and rethinking of old values in the

United States, and zoos became part of that revolution. More consideration was given to conservation, the treatment of animals and the role of zoos.

Dr. Heini Hediger, director of the Basel Zoo in Switzerland (1944–1953) and then of the Zurich Zoo (1954 to the time of his death), had a major influence on zoo design and the way humans provided for the animals in their care. Through his observations of animals in the wild and in zoos, he determined that the essential physical, psychological and social needs of species could be met even in a space smaller than their natural habitat. But it was critical to the welfare of the animals in captivity to have those needs met. Dr. Hediger made the comment in *Man and Animal in the Zoo* that, "The standard by which a zoo animal is judged should be according to the life it leads in the wild."

During the 1960s, we were learning a great deal more about animals in their natural habitat. Field biologists like Jane Goodall and George Schaller taught us about the behavior of animals. In large part it was now up to zoos to teach the public about the wonders of the animal world. Education departments in zoos became common and took on a bigger role, providing classes. Docents, or volunteer departments, also became part of the zoo team focusing on the education of zoo visitors.

In the 1970s, as people learned more about standards of animal care, there was an increasing outcry about the treatment of zoo animals. Animal welfare organizations demonstrated against zoos. The Humane Society of the United States, one of the largest organizations in this country to monitor the care and treatment of animals, wrote guidelines for zoos to draw attention to the needs of the animals. Some people demanded the closing of all zoos; others wanted changes made in animal care.

Zoo professionals, the people who care for the animals every day, also looked for ways to create higher standards for all zoos. They took on the responsibility of monitoring their own operations by forming the American Association of Zoological Parks and Aquariums (AAZPA) which is now known as the AZA (American Zoo and Aquarium Association).

During this period in the early 1970s, the AZA recognized that collections of animals were valuable for entertainment only if it served to educate the public and only if studying the animals in the zoo would benefit the world scientifically.

Something else was changing drastically within the zoo community. Rather than competition, there was a new spirit of cooperation among zoos. The better zoos worked together to improve conditions for their animal collections, to provide educational opportunities for the public and, most important, to conserve and protect animals still in their natural habitats.

There was more research being done on wild animals, more conferences and more exchanges of people and information among zoos, universities and countries.

Just as science and medical technology were leaping forward for humans, great advances were being made for animals too. Captive animals could receive excellent health care, eat appropriate diets, breed more successfully and live in better conditions.

In the 1970s, two landscape architects, Jon Coe and Grant Jones, along with Dennis Paulson and David Hancocks, director at the time, developed the concept of "landscape immersion" exhibits when they designed the gorilla habitat in the Woodland Park Zoo in Seattle, Washington. Going beyond Hagenbeck's concept, these exhibits put the animals into a naturalistic environment complete with plants, rockwork and often other animals. More important, they brought the visitor into the environment. In immersion exhibits,

"WILD KINGDOM"

On January 6, 1963, a new television show was put on the air with Marlin Perkins, a zoo director, as host: "Wild Kingdom." Co-host Jim Fowler says that in the early days they did not think they would have enough material to get through the first year. Yet the show continued for 329 episodes until 1991, six years after Marlin Perkins's death. Perkins's efforts to enable people to look beyond their homes into the wild kingdom spanned thirty years.

tricks of design make the visitor feel as though he is part of the gorilla's environment. The birds fly overhead; the visitor is surrounded by the sounds of the jungle and is brushed by the vegetation.

The idea is that once you have been there in the habitat, feeling the environment much as the animal does, you will understand it on a more visceral or basic level. And if you understand it, you will care about the animals and their environment.

In the 1980s, zoos benefited from the spending spree of the decade. More and better exhibit techniques were developed. New materials were created, and old materials, like concrete, were used in new ways to build zoo habitats complete with trees, ponds and mud banks. Hagenbeck's idea of naturalistic habitats went yet another step.

Now, in the 1990s, zoos around the world are taking on another role in their evolution, reaching out beyond their acres in the city to help protect animals and habitats in the wild.

In many cases, zoos are the only places where some animals survive. These animals include the Micronesian kingfisher, a species of bird which became extinct on the island of Guam when humans introduced the brown tree snake, which ate the birds' eggs. There are currently only sixty Micronesian kingfishers in zoos. None survive in the wild.

Now the AZA insists that the priorities of their mission must be reversed; conservation, education and scientific study must come before recreation.

The progression has happened naturally. Zoos are in a position to protect animals, both in the wild and in zoos. There are already rare animals breeding successfully in the protected environment of zoos. Endangered animals are being protected in the wild. The small world community of zoos is working cooperatively to protect the population of animals.

Pygmy chimpanzees are an example of this cooperation. In the wild, they survive only in one small pocket in the African country of Zaire, and a total of eighty-five live in several small groups in zoos around the world. They must be managed and conserved as one population if they are to survive at all.

In the 1990s, zoos are in an excellent position to educate. In North America, more people visit zoos every year than attend all professional sporting events combined including football, baseball, basketball and hockey games. That is over 100.8 million people. Worldwide, zoos and aquariums have a collective annual visitation of over 800 million people, making them one of the largest conservation networks on earth. If zoos are able to reach those people with a conservation message, they can have a dramatic impact on changing the public's attitude toward wildlife.

To that end, zoos have recently joined to write *The World Zoo Conservation Strategy*, an eighty-page strategy to help achieve global

---

In 1924, the directors of zoological gardens belonged to the American Institute of Park Executives. Then, in 1966, zoo directors became a part of the National Recreation and Parks Association.

But, as zoos changed, so too did the needs of the professionals. There were conflicts between the parks departments and the AZA, whose needs and focus were different. Finally it became clear that they must be separate organizations.

In 1972, the AZA pulled away to become an independent organization. The members, directors of zoological gardens, made their mission "to pursue and further expand conservation, science and education."

Zoos around the world are in a position to protect animals, both in the wild and in captivity. There are many rare animals breeding successfully in the protected environment of zoos and many still being protected in the wild by the zoo community. The small world community of zoos is working cooperatively to protect the population of animals.

Pygmy chimpanzees are an example of this cooperation. In the wild they survive only in one small pocket in the African country of Zaire, and a total of eighty-five live in several small groups in zoos around the world. The zoo community has taken aggressive steps in managing and preserving this small population.

conservation goals. The document comes from two years of discussion led by IUDZG (International Union of Directors of Zoological Gardens, the world zoo organization) and CBSG (Captive Breeding Specialist Group).

Briefly, the strategy emphasizes three areas where zoos and aquariums can reach conservation goals:

1. Supporting the conservation of endangered species and ecosystems.
2. Offering professional support and facilities to increase scientific knowledge that will benefit conservation.
3. Promoting an increase in public awareness of the need for conservation.

Although it is a considerable force in conservation efforts, this strategy should be complementary to and integrated with other fields of conservation activity. The World Wildlife Fund and the IUCN (International Union for the Conservation of Nature) support *The World Zoo Conservation Strategy*.

In the twenty-first century, zoos may no longer be confined to a park or a country; the zoos of the world will create and protect wide varieties of animals and plants in vast habitats—all the different bits of the complicated web of life.

Chapter Four
DESIGN, CONSTRUCTION AND ENRICHMENT

In early menageries, the visitors would look down into a pit to see animals like bears and alligators—perhaps reflecting the attitude of humans toward animals then. Now, zoo evolution places the visitor as a guest entering the world of animals. Dressing up chimpanzees and putting them in chairs to sip tea like humans—as was done in the past—is certainly not an appropriate thing for chimpanzees to do. There is a middle ground where we can respect the animal and meet its requirements while still finding it an interesting member of another species.

In planning the exhibits, many things must be carefully considered, just as if the planning were for a house: heat, air conditioning, light, drains, faucets, noise, smell. The needs of the animals, their keepers and the public must be taken into account.

Beyond such seemingly humane concerns, though, today's zoo exhibit should be judged by how well it replicates the animal's life in the wild. What field biologists learn by observing animals in their natural habitats benefits animals in zoos. Exhibit designers often travel to distant parts of the world to explore natural habitats themselves. Exhibit designer and landscape architect Jon Coe traveled to the African nations of Zaire, Cameroon and Rwanda before designing gorilla habitats in a number of zoos around the United States. Creating a balanced exhibit often requires years of planning. Animal behavior must be understood, as well as the particular space requirements for various species.

In the World of Birds at the Bronx Zoo/Wildlife Conservation Park, no glass or wire keeps the birds in their exhibits. The visitor stands in a darkened hallway, looking directly into the bright, well-planned exhibit. This open expanse is possible because the designers understood that the birds prefer to stay where there is light and food in the exhibit rather than flying out into the dark unknown.

Jon Coe with
Zoo Atlanta group
visiting mountain
gorillas in Rwanda
as research for
gorilla exhibit.

The resulting gorilla
exhibit at Zoo
Atlanta created after
field studies
in Rwanda. The
exhibit attempts
to set up the same
relationship
between gorillas
and people
as designers
experienced in
the wild.

The gorillas' night quarters at the Woodland Park Zoo.

Rhino and giraffes— a hidden barrier between giraffes and the black rhino at Zoo Atlanta gives the impression of animals roaming as might be seen in the wild.

Kenya impala herd at the San Diego Wild Animal Park. Since an exhibit is home to animals, proper planning of space is essential to allow animals to roam free or to retreat for privacy from other animals or the public.

SPACE

Exhibits may need height for climbers, depths for turtle pools or burrows for prairie dogs. Since an exhibit is home, the animals need places where they can retreat for privacy from other animals or the public: nooks, logs, rocks, branches. A gibbon will need to brachiate (swing its long arms to move from place to place), so it must have branches or ropes. Leaf-cutter ants require lots of soil, with precise temperatures and humidity, for their tunnels.

Greater consideration is now given even to night quarters—traditionally, basic bars and tile—because animals spend half their time there, after all, and the off-exhibit areas are important for their well-being.

Safety is a big consideration. The animals must be protected from both accidents in the exhibit and the viewing public—and the area must be safe for the visitors as well.

VISUAL TRICKS

Experimenting with scale models, designers find ways to keep people from seeing too many other people across the exhibit, perhaps with the inclusion of a strategically placed boulder or a curve in the pathway, to encourage the feeling that the visitor is alone in the habitat with the animals.

There are ways to make it appear that predator and prey are in the same exhibit, when in actuality, wire, moats, glass or boulders keep them apart. With pergolas, or viewing blinds, and false ceilings, the focus of visitors' attention is kept on the exhibit, not wandering up to the sprinkler system.

It may seem like a lucky coincidence that the python is always lying on the branch close to the glass but it is likely that there is a heating coil built into the "branch." Snakes like warmth, so the snake seeks the spot. There are other tricks to keep animals visible in large or heavily planted exhibits: cool rocks, food dispensers built into a tree, enrichment activities and training.

SOUND AND TOUCH

Sometimes sound recordings are used so that the visitor can "hear" the environment as well as see and smell it. Sound designers travel to the real habitat to record bird songs, rain, insects buzzing and leaves rustling. At the San

Diego Zoo, the recordings at the new gorilla exhibit are so sophisticated that the volume is adjusted for the number of people who walk past the sensor hidden in the bushes.

Some exhibits produce mist or rainfall every once in a while to add to the ambiance. Even the ground the visitor will stand on is considered in the overall design.

CONSTRUCTION

Plumbers, electricians, painters, carpenters and even computer experts must be available to repair and build in the zoo. If the heat goes off in the middle of the winter, someone must fix it immediately before the tropical animals get cold and sick.

Some zoos have their own staff to build exhibits. Others bring in outside consultants and craftsmen. A whole industry has grown around exhibit construction. There are companies that work with the zoo staff to design and build naturalistic exhibits. They use old materials, like concrete, in new ways to build artificial trees or riverbanks or new materials, such as a rubberlike compound that can be molded and painted to look like bark and still withstand the activity of curious and strong monkeys living in the habitat.

IMMERSION EXHIBITS

Is a tree a tree even if it is made of epoxy? What does the proboscis monkey sitting on it think? Can you tell if it is concrete or bark? In

Building an immersion exhibit.

many zoos today, you cannot see the difference.

Artificial materials can be used to create tropical exhibits as well as deserts and the Arctic, whatever human imagination can come up with. New technology allows constantly better exhibits. Construction materials such as concrete, steel bars, epoxy and paint are turned into trees, bark, roots, vines and lichens.

Aviaries can be built with nearly invisible black netting. Piano wire is used instead of bars or wire mesh in front of some cages. At

To recreate nature is no easy task. It is slow work, demanding great patience. One woman taking on such tasks is Jonquil Rock.

To her came the challenge of building a tropical rain forest in the Bronx. Working with the Larson Company, an exhibit design firm, under the guidance of William Conway, the general director of the Wildlife Conservation Society, Jonquil and her team created trees and rocks from wire, Gunite and paint. Over several years of experimentation with the techniques, a rain forest emerged, JungleWorld, the Indonesian rain forest at Bronx Zoo/Wildlife Conservation Park. Without very close inspection, it is difficult to tell what is real and what is artificial. Jonquil and her crew handpainted all the artificial bark of thirty-five trees in JungleWorld, some standing fifty feet tall.

Jonquil's husband, Dave Rock, is a noted muralist able to paint the concrete or plaster walls of exhibits and turn them into a detailed panorama of jungle, mountains or desert. Jonquil and Dave work together creating murals as backdrops to exhibits in zoos and museums.

Finished JungleWorld exhibit—
a gibbon in the trees.

the Lincoln Park Zoo, the glass that separates the visitor from the one thousand pounds of a charging adult male gorilla is several layers of 1 5/8-inch-thick laminated security glass. New techniques in glass design also make possible transparent pools where penguins and polar bears can be watched.

Instead of bars or barbed wire, electrified "hot wire" encircles many enclosures to keep the animals in. After the first mild shock, few animals will try to get past it a second time.

Add real plants, real soil, water, sound effects and a touch of imagination and you have an immersion exhibit.

What all these elements lead to is the latest in zoo exhibit design, allowing the visitors to feel as though they are really in the habitat with the animals. In the case of the Wildlife Conservation Society's JungleWorld, that means right in the middle of an Indonesian rain forest.

JungleWorld is a huge building filled with towering trees (real and artificial), waterfalls, tropical humidity, the sounds of tropical birds and all the wildlife which is natural to that area of the world. It is very different from standing in front of a cage.

This concept was first named "landscape immersion" by Jon Coe, Grant Jones and David Hancocks in their 1976 design for the Woodland Park Zoo in Seattle, Washington. It is the kind of exhibit concept that a zoo like the Arizona-Sonora Desert Museum created

by taking the visitor into the habitat of the indigenous wildlife. Other zoo directors, like George Rabb and William Conway, had the vision for such exhibits before the technology was available and have created some remarkable exhibits since new construction techniques have evolved.

You may not see the likes of the Bronx JungleWorld in every zoo. JungleWorld cost more than $10 million in 1989. Currently, it costs an average of $450–$550 per square foot to build an exhibit in a large city. It is estimated that $1.2 billion is spent annually on capital improvements for zoos and aquariums in the United States.

Seeing animals in an immersion exhibit accomplishes several things. It is more natural and therefore interesting to the animal and it helps humans appreciate the diverse environments the animals live in. In an immersion exhibit, you "feel" the habitat. If you feel involved, it is more likely that you will care about the animals and habitats you see.

SNOW LEOPARD EXHIBIT

In the early 1990s, a new exhibit was opened for the snow leopards at Bronx Zoo/Wildlife Conservation Park. The snow leopards have been breeding very well at the zoo but are endangered in the wild.

General curator James G. Doherty worked with keepers, exhibit designers, graphics curator John Gwynne, architects and field biologists who know these animals well.

Snow leopards are solitary cats, except for mating. In the wild, they have huge territories. But in the zoo, they do not need so much range because they do not have to hunt for food. Nevertheless, they need an interesting space, with lots of nooks and crannies to jump and rest in. The designers understood that the snow leopard can leap fifty feet after a target. They didn't want the target to be a visitor.

Although it looks like one large exhibit, it is actually several, so that several animals can be on display, including birds that live in the territory of the snow leopard.

The exhibit needed to be a place that

Model of snow leopard exhibit at the Bronx Zoo/Wildlife Conservation Park.

Snow leopard in snow leopard
exhibit at the Bronx Zoo/Wildlife
Conservation Park.

would remain relatively cool all year long, a basic necessity for animals adapted to life high in the mountains of Tibet. A hillside facing east was selected because it stays cool.

Built into the hill are their "bedrooms," sixteen holding cages where they go at night out of the main exhibit. Some animals rotate in and out. Not all the same animals are in the exhibit every day. There are also four maternity dens for mothers and their cubs.

To keep the animals from escaping, a dark wire netting is used which blends into the habitat.

ENVIRONMENTAL ENRICHMENT

It seems incredible that some animals are still forced to live in bare boxes, with nothing to do hour after hour, year after year.

Animals in such cruel cages can be seen pacing back and forth or rocking. Any kind of abnormal repetitive behavior like this is called a stereotype, and it helps reduce the anxiety or frustration of a situation. When people are nervous, they often pace back and forth, bite fingernails or twirl hair with their fingers.

Fortunately, taking into account their natural behaviors, humans are figuring out ways to provide zoo animals with interesting things to do which stimulate them and help prevent boredom and emotional problems.

Much of environmental enrichment is based on food. For most animals in the wild, searching for food is an activity that takes up most of the day. Being fed by keepers once or twice a day is unnatural and leaves the animals with little to do for the rest of the day.

Some animals evolved to hunt may eat but once every few days. To keep animals physically and emotionally healthy, the provision of food must be adapted to meet their needs as closely as possible.

Enrichment can be as simple as scattering seeds in the hay of a monkey enclosure so the monkeys can forage, giving elephants browse (branches and leaves) to munch on during the day or hiding food for small cats like civets and marguay around the cage.

Cats naturally are hunters. They have evolved to spend a great deal of their time watching and stalking. If they cannot do this, they start to pace. Dr. Kathy Carlstead, a biologist who has done research on environmental enrichment with many zoo animals, found that they pace considerably less when they can "hunt" for hidden food items. She collected urine samples to compare hormone levels for stress in cats fed in barren cages to those in cats whose food was hidden at different times of the day. The simple act of finding food behind branches stopped pacing behavior for several days.

The Copenhagen Zoo in Denmark has put together a catalog of behavioral-enrichment ideas for some fifty species. Dr. David Shepardson, a British zoologist working at the Washington Park Zoo in Oregon, has also compiled comprehensive ideas for enrichment, all based on natural behaviors.

There are many possibilities for environmental enrichment including: artificial termite nests for chimps which allow them to use a stick as a tool to get at yogurt, honey or peanut butter in a narrow tube; "curtains" of

Many zoos are now conscious of the need to recycle. They can turn the tons of manure into "ZooDoo," which can be used on gardens. At the Akron Zoo, the benches and picnic tables are made out of recycled plastics. Some zoos have built co-generation plants to use the energy created by one source of power, perhaps steam, to heat a building and to power an electrical generator.

A bear at Zoo Atlanta uses a tree stump to scratch its back. Simple structures help to create a more natural and enriching environment for the animal.

Top: Bornean orangutan (male) at the San Diego Zoo digging for honey.

Bottom: A simple barrel provides environmental enrichment for the Siberian tigers at the Bronx Zoo/Wildife Conservation Park by giving them something to investigate.

rope for big cats, tigers and leopards to use as scratching posts; hides for snow leopards to drag around; mealworms tucked into branches and crevices for anteaters to discover.

Just giving chimps a coconut can keep them occupied for a long time. They have to work to get it open, once open they can enjoy the meat and milk, then they may turn it into a cup, or a hat, or chase each other to get it. Given the right material—hay, branches, even burlap bags—chimpanzees will make nests just like they do in the wild. Strawberries frozen in an ice block give polar bears treats to lick for an hour or so. Cheetahs need to chase, to sprint as they are designed to do. Someone came up with the idea of using the same kind of pulley system with a fake rabbit that is used to train greyhounds for cheetahs to chase.

SOCIAL ENRICHMENT

In good zoos today, social animals live in groups, herd animals in herds and flock birds in flocks. Chimpanzees, like people, are social animals. They need to be with others of their

Top: Polar bear mother with cub—when possible it is preferred to keep families together.

Bottom: A lowland gorilla family at the San Diego Zoo.

Gorillas in the wild must eat all day long to get enough nutrition from the vegetation they eat. In the zoo, they have a very nutritious diet and cannot snack all day on high-calorie food just to keep busy or they would quickly become overweight. Introducing browse, or vegetation for them to munch on throughout the day, keeps away boredom and improves their health by providing roughage they need in their diets. Also, chewing on leaves and branches keeps their teeth and gums clean.

species. Infants must have role models to become successful chimpanzees. They learn from their mothers what to eat, how to care for their own babies and how to behave with dominant animals. Without examples to learn from, they do not become successful members of the species.

Primates are not the only such social animals. Flamingos live naturally in immense flocks of thousands of birds. They seem to require the presence of others to trigger mating behavior. At the Wildfowl and Wetlands Trust in Slimbridge, Gloucestershire, England, the tiny flock of thirty birds was giving no indication that they would breed. It was impossible to install a flock of adequate size to stimulate natural behaviors, so a mirror was placed in the exhibit to try and trick the birds. Now, they "see" twice the number of flamingos as are actually in the flock and seem to be stimulated enough at least to begin their courtship ritual—marching around in tight formation and braying loudly.

It is often reported that in a new exhibit or with a new group of animals, the "honeymoon phenomenon" occurs. Animals that had not bred do so all of a sudden. Three baby gorillas were born in the first fourteen months (gestation is eight months) at the new gorilla complex at Zoo Atlanta.

Zoos have taught us that some behaviors we assumed were rigid are not. For example, there have been interesting observations by keepers of orangutans, the great apes from Indonesia. In the wild, they are solitary animals. Yet, in the zoo, they tend to live very well in social groups, even past their adolescent years. The reason is thought to be that there is plenty of food in the zoo, unlike in their natural habitat, the quickly disappearing forests of Indonesia. In the wild, it is advantageous to travel alone in order to get the best from the fruit trees.

A flock of flamingos at Sea World in San Diego—flamingos live naturally in immense flocks of thousands of birds. They seem to require the presence of others to trigger mating behavior.

In the wild orangutans are solitary animals, yet, in a zoo, they tend to live very well in social groups.

Chapter Five
WHO'S WHO AT THE ZOO?

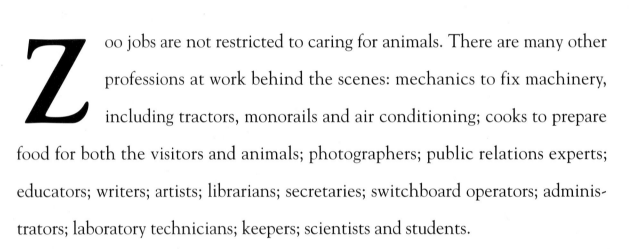

Zoo jobs are not restricted to caring for animals. There are many other professions at work behind the scenes: mechanics to fix machinery, including tractors, monorails and air conditioning; cooks to prepare food for both the visitors and animals; photographers; public relations experts; educators; writers; artists; librarians; secretaries; switchboard operators; administrators; laboratory technicians; keepers; scientists and students.

ANIMAL KEEPER

The animals depend on the keepers for their daily care and food, a clean exhibit and for making sure that they are well. The keeper must be tuned into the moods of the animal. Often, by the time obvious symptoms appear in sick animals, especially wild animals, their lives may already be in danger. The keepers must know the animals well enough to detect any change in behavior or appetite immediately and report it to the veterinarian.

A keeper should get a close look at every animal in his or her care at least twice a day. One way to do this is to have the animals come inside, or into a "bedroom," every night. The animals are fed in their night quarters, so they are usually eager to go in. They are observed again in the morning before they go outside or into the exhibit.

Some zoos have a "team approach" to different areas of the zoo. The team includes keepers, gardeners, teachers and people who maintain the building. In this way, many people know individual animals and feel responsible for an exhibit area.

If an animal is sick or about to give birth, the keepers set up watches around the clock to be on alert for complications that could require a veterinarian. Around-the-clock watches may also take place when new animals have arrived at the zoo or an animal is introduced to a new mate or herd. Often, there is little a human can do to prevent a fight or injury, but by knowing the animals well and supervising such events, the keepers

Keeper at the San Diego Zoo trimming the toenails and callous pads of an African elephant.

Keeper at the National Zoo simulating fruit trees. The fruit is being hidden in the golden lion tamarin exhibit, where the animal will have to search and acquire the fruit on its own, as it would in the wild.

assure that things go as smoothly as possible.

On rare occasions, keepers have been killed by animals in their care. No matter how close or friendly or trusting the animals seem, they are still wild.

Every zoo has its own rules and philosophy about handling the animals. People generally have strong emotions about their relationships with those in their care. Some feel that under no circumstances should animals as powerful as elephants be handled or touched.

Others feel that there is no way that an animal as intelligent and sensitive as an elephant should not be touched. There should only be limited contact. Both sides have evidence to support their views.

Training animals has become a very important part of a keeper's job in some zoos. This does not mean training like in the era of animal shows: chimpanzees walking a tightrope or sipping tea. Rather, it uses psychology and positive reinforcement to "shape" the action

A keeper at the Phoenix Zoo noticed that Ruby, a nine-year-old African elephant, would use a stick or grasses to make patterns in the sand. The keeper gave Ruby big rods of colored chalk and paper to see what she would do. Ruby seems to love it. In her big trunk she carefully holds the chalk—she chooses the colors—and draws on the paper. She is careful to keep the paper from moving by gently placing her foot on the corner. If the paper rips, she smooths it down again with her trunk. Money from the sale of her drawings goes to support the zoo.

To have an elephant draw may not be exactly what a zoo is about, but it shows that keepers can be perceptive and provide the animals with new experiences. This kind of activity also helps to educate the zoogoers, making them more interested and appreciative of the animals' abilities.

Pat Sass with baby chimpanzee.

of the animal. Teaching a young giraffe to go willingly into a crate is an example of how the animal's behavior can be shaped. The giraffe is given a food treat each time it approaches the crate—positive reinforcement. Before long, the animal is comfortable going close to the crate and eventually will step inside, lured by a reward. This process may take weeks. The giraffe may never have to go into the crate, but if he does have to travel to another zoo, or must be confined for medical care, the training has prepared him. Entering into the crate is routine, not the stressful, dangerous situation it would be if he were forced inside.

At Metro Toronto Zoo, a gorilla was caring wonderfully for her first infant. The mother held it, protected it and put it to her breast to nurse. But unfortunately, she did not produce enough milk to adequately feed her baby. The keepers had to take the baby away from her and hand-feed it by bottle. When the baby was strong enough and able to eat other food, it was returned to the mother. The next time she became pregnant, the zoo did not want to risk again the trauma of separating mother and baby. They prepared. During the pregnancy, the keepers trained her to hold a bottle of prepared formula and "feed" it to a doll. The gorilla's behavior was shaped to feed her newborn from a bottle, if again she did not have enough milk.

Keepers also work to provide activities for the animals. Living in the wild, an animal must find its own food, protect its territory, secure a mate and raise its young. Every day is filled with activity, problems and needs. In a zoo, the animal is provided everything—food, shelter and often a mate. Boredom is often a problem. Especially for the more intelligent animals, like the great apes or elephants, the keepers think of ways to enrich their environment. The animals are given

It was not until about twenty-five years ago that women could become keepers at the Lincoln Park Zoo. The work was considered too hard. Pat Sass was one of the first three women to take the keeper course. Two of them are still there.

something to do to fill the hours of the day, to provide an outlet for natural behaviors and to stimulate their minds.

Logs or ropes may be put into a jaguar exhibit to satisfy the need the big cats have to sharpen their claws. The logs and ropes are used for play also. A sunbear may spend all day digging around in the soil searching for the meal worms the keeper has scattered there. Since a primary function for an animal is finding something to eat, much of the enrichment provided by the keepers revolves around food. This is an area of their work in which keepers can be very creative.

A keeper has to be consistent with the animals. Through positive conditioning, the animals know what to expect every day and develop trust in the people they have to depend on. A keeper at the National Zoo has gained so much trust from the orangutans in his care that a mother orangutan will hold her infant up to the bars so that he can give the baby an injection. This helps avoid the stress of tranquilizing the mother and upsetting the baby.

The role of the zookeeper has changed. Centuries ago, the job went to any unskilled worker—like the keeper at the Tower of London. Today, most of the better zoos employ individuals with higher degrees in biology, zoology or other related subjects to deal with the increased complexity involved in caring properly for captive animals.

Over the past twenty years, keepers have become more respected for their knowledge and contribution to the understanding of animals.

Sometimes, keepers go into the field (the wild) to observe animals or help with the training of keepers in other countries. North American keepers have their own organization, the American Association of Zoo Keepers (AAZK). The members share information, hold workshops and promote conservation programs.

VETERINARIAN

It was not until the 1940s that veterinary medicine became an important consideration for zoos. It was often easier and cheaper to get new animals from the wild than to treat sick ones in captivity. Also, little was known about exotic animals. Zoo vets often consulted with circuses about the care of the animals.

In 1946, at the annual meeting of the American Veterinary Medical Association (AVMA), a handful of veterinarians working part-time in zoos set up their own organization which came to be known as the American Association of Zoo Veterinarians (AAZV).

It was not until 1954 that the first full-time zoo vet in the United States was hired at the National Zoo. By 1992, there were about 125. Some zoos also have training programs for veterinary students wishing to specialize in the care of exotic animals.

The AAZK has started environmental projects all around the country and the world. An annual "Bowling for Rhinos" program raises money for the conservation of white rhinos. They have organized cleanups on Earth Day. Keepers from the six zoos in the San Francisco area began a program to raise money to buy acres of rain forest. They turned parking meters into "environmental meters"—a jaguar or tapir jumps up instead of the red time-expired flag. Jaguars are popping up all over the zoos, raising enough money so far to buy more than one hundred acres of rain forest in Costa Rica through the Nature Conservancy, an organization that buys up land in order to preserve its natural state.

William Hornaday, first director of the Bronx Zoo, operating on a Mexican grizzly bear in 1904. Example of an early zoo hospital.

A Siberian tiger receiving a dental check-up at the San Diego Zoo.

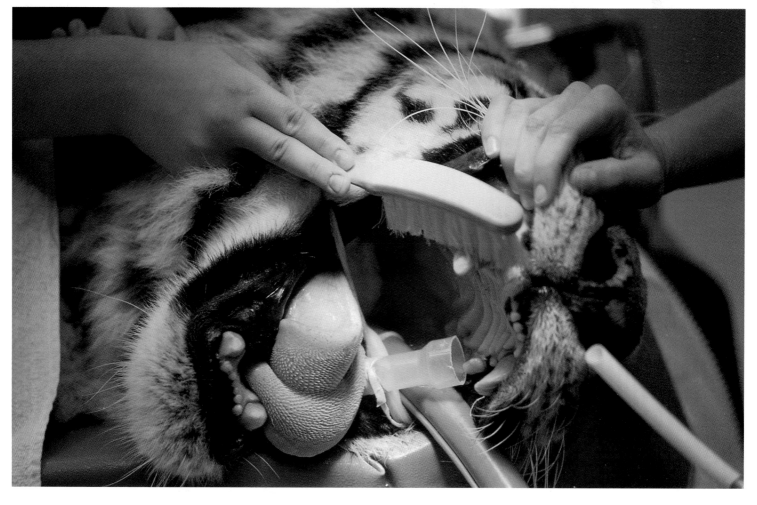

Most zoos have some kind of health-care team including a veterinarian, laboratory technician and pathologist. Depending on the size and sophistication of the zoo, there may also be a geneticist who helps plan breeding programs.

When the first vets became part of the team of zoo professionals, their work was mostly guesswork. They were skilled in treating domestic animals such as cats, dogs, horses and sheep but knew nothing about tigers, rhinoceros, cranes, pythons or gorillas. Today, with experience and communication between the growing number of exotic animal veterinarians, the care of zoo animals has become extremely sophisticated.

Some zoos have X-ray equipment and surgical suites (often big enough for an elephant). The Bronx Zoo opened the first zoo hospital in 1916.

Zoo veterinarians concern themselves not only with preventive care, making certain that animals stay in the best of health, but they must be trained to do complicated surgery and dental work, predict pregnancy, do embryo transplants and many of the techniques which are critical for the survival of endangered species. They must be experts in animal behavior, nutrition, birth and death.

To become a veterinarian is a long educational process. The college program includes much the same preparation as pre-med coursework. The graduate program in veterinary medicine continues for four more years. Like medical doctors, veterinarians also do a residency, seeking work in a zoo or with exotic animals in another setting to gain experience on the job.

Even if a zoo does not have a full-time veterinarian, it is likely to have other medical employees, such as laboratory technicians. These professionals are trained to analyze blood and fecal samples and do other studies to help in determining the health of the animal. They are generally responsible for nursing an ailing animal back to health.

A pathologist may also be part of the zoo medical team, to perform autopsies to learn more about the cause of death and to discover basic information about the species.

ANIMAL-PATIENT DIAGNOSIS

Since animals cannot tell us where it hurts or how long they have had a queasy stomach, humans must use observation, guesswork, medical tests and experience to diagnose an illness in a zoo animal. The keepers will work with the health-care team by observing the animal. Perhaps a new member in the group is upsetting her and she is not eating. Moving her to a private location for a time might give her the peace she needs. Lab tests may be done; the animal may have to be tranquilized for a full examination to find out why she won't get up, seems listless or does not become pregnant.

Some analyses are nonintrusive (information can be gathered without the animal knowing). A urine sample can be collected from under the cage to check hormone levels to find out if the animal is pregnant. Examination of feces will reveal if the animal has a parasite. Some animals can even be trained to cooperate in a medical examination. Most elephants are conditioned to stand still and allow blood to be drawn from a vein behind an ear. It is much better for the elephant to be trained to allow this than to stress her and tranquilize her every time a sample is needed. Some chimpanzees will present their arms for blood to be drawn. A food reward is enough to put up with what to them seems to be a minor inconvenience.

But most animals won't cooperate so neatly, and it becomes essential to tranquilize them. And often when animals are moved, they must be tranquilized or sedated. Fortunately, veterinary medicine has developed tranquilizers for exotic animals. (When animals had to be physically restrained for treatment, it was very stressful to the animal and sometimes dangerous for the humans. Now, one injection immobilizes the animal, or "puts him to sleep," while the treatment is carried out.)

It took years to perfect these effective, safe tranquilizing drugs, since dosage and reaction are different for every species and even for different individuals. Dosage is critical. The unexpected must still be anticipated. A hippo may run to the water's edge and collapse with his head in the water, drowning.

Getting the drug into the animal has its possible pitfalls. Usually it has to be done with a dart fired from a gun or with a "pole syringe," a long pole with a dart on the end. The dart should go right into a muscled place like the thigh or rump. Modern drugs and equipment in the hands of trained and experienced medical personnel have made these procedures reliable.

As important as tranquilizing the animal is bringing it to consciousness. New drugs allow the animal to wake up quickly and without serious aftereffects. This is especially important in the wild or even in the zoo—because if an animal is to return to its group quickly, it must behave normally to be reaccepted by the others. There have been cases where the animal behaved so strangely, weaving and staggering as it came out of anesthesia, that members of its own group turned on it.

Tranquilizing is not to be repeated casually. Therefore, the veterinarian wants to be sure to collect all possible information while the animal is unconscious. After attending to whatever required the immobilization in the first place—a wound, illness or medical procedure—the team works quickly to take blood and measurements and to check teeth, ears and eyes. So, for example, when a male gorilla is tranquilized, semen may also be taken for research.

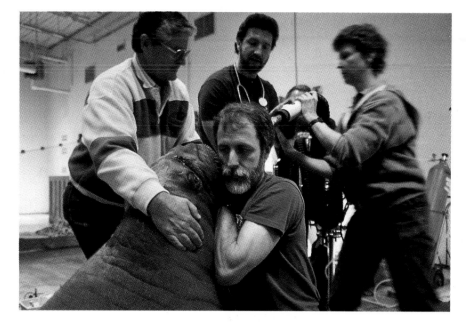

Top: Team collecting data on a tranquilized walrus.

Two methods for drawing blood from an animal. Center: this method of attaining blood can be very stressful for the animal. Such close contact and the manipulation of the entire animal can be very intrusive and place both the animal and health care team in danger. Bottom: Nonintrusive analysis is less stressful for the animal. Many elephants can be trained to stand still and allow blood to be drawn from a vein behind the ear. There is an ongoing discussion about how much elephants should be handled.

ARRIVING AT THE ZOO

There are two ways animals arrive at the zoo: by birth to a zoo animal or from outside—another zoo or an animal dealer.

Unless they are born in the zoo, new animals are kept in quarantine. Quarantine is often many months long and is necessary to make certain they are not carrying any disease. During quarantine, the animals have every aspect of their health checked out. It gives the animals a chance to get used to their new surroundings and the keepers a chance to get to know the animals.

In most cases, zoos try to leave infants with their mothers from birth. Sometimes this is not possible because the mother rejects the baby or the little one is ill. Most zoos have some sort of a nursery, often like human nurseries, complete with incubators, cribs, soft rugs, toys and even a rocking chair. Baby gorillas or chimpanzees need the comfort of another primate body, even if it is not that of their natural mother. A human holds and feeds and plays with the baby. In the best of cases, there are several primate infants in the nursery so that they can play together and have continual social contact.

Sometimes there are lion cubs, young hippos or gazelles, all requiring tender care and watchful eyes. Of course, there are less snuggly animals in the nursery too: reptile eggs hatching in the incubators or young birds that require feeding every hour by the human staff.

From the moment an animal arrives at the zoo—from within or without—its medical care begins. Technicians track the animal's weight, medications, behavior, diet, appearance and general health.

Primates need the comfort of another body.

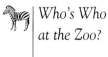
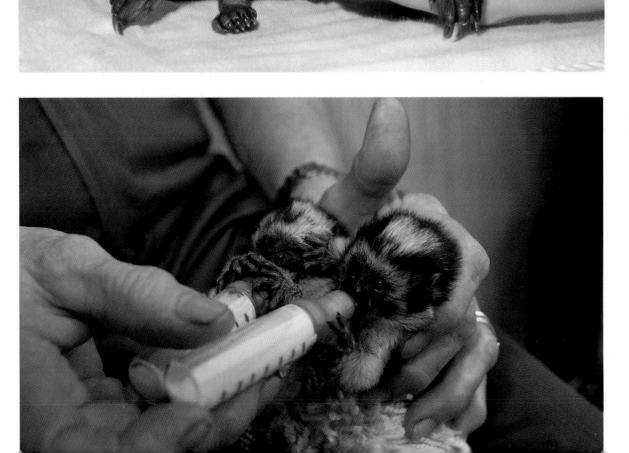

Top: Baby orangutan at the San Diego Zoo. Most zoos have a nursery, often like human nurseries, complete with incubators, cribs, soft rugs and toys.

Middle: Newly born aardvark in an incubator at the San Diego Zoo.

Bottom: Keeper feeding two baby tamarins.

Top: New baby tiger in nursery incubator.

Middle: Keeper at the Bronx Zoo/Wildlife Conservation Park feeding a baby hippo.

The nursery is a wonderful place for zoo staff to work. It is very special to bottle-feed a baby hippo or change the diaper of a chimpanzee. But it is very demanding of time and of emotions. Handraising an animal leads to a great attachment, and no matter how wonderful it is to see them join others of their species, it can be hard to let go.

Docents are volunteers who are available throughout the zoo to answer questions about particular animals or exhibits. Usually zoos cannot afford to have many teachers or paid people to help explain exhibits or animals. The docents make it possible for more visitors to have questions answered.

Docents take many months of classes to learn about the animals in the zoo. They offer a great deal of interesting and fun information about particular animals and exhibits. They may help you see things in the exhibit you might otherwise have missed.... "See that female monkey sitting up in the tree? Her name is Rhubarb. She is holding a three-day-old baby, her first." Probably you would have missed seeing the tiny hands clutching the mother's fur. But when it is pointed out to you, it makes your zoo visit much more special.

LEAVING THE ZOO

After death, a necropsy is performed. The necropsy is important in helping veterinarians to determine the extent and possible origin of diseases which may have caused the animal's death. Understanding why the animal died often can be useful in the care of the living.

Currently, there is an international computer program being put together to document all medical situations having to do with elephants in North American zoos, so that all zoos have access to it.

Dr. William Karesh started his career as a biologist, focusing on animal behavior. After he got his degree, he went to work at the National Zoo and then on to veterinary school. He was interested in the challenge of exotic animals.

With his veterinary training, he spent several years at the San Diego Zoo and then at the Seattle Woodland Park Zoo, where he started a research and conservation field program. He now works with the Wildlife Conservation Society as their field veterinarian.

Now, Dr. Karesh can be found dodging enraged bull forest elephants, trying to solve the mystery of five hundred hippos dying of "black leg" or training veterinarians from Indonesia, Zaire or Brazil for medical care and management in the field.

NUTRITIONIST

The job of a zoo nutritionist, a fairly new one at zoos, is to find out what foods work to keep animals in top condition. It is hard to imagine that back in the 1920s people really believed that a chimpanzee could live on sausages and beer. (Chimps given such a diet died.)

Nutritionists study the vitamins and minerals each species needs and in what combinations and what foods contain those nutrients. They need to know what quantities of vitamin E a rhino needs and from what food sources the rhino can get the nutrients in proper amounts.

Nutritionists collect and analyze what the animals would naturally eat in the wild. Sometimes they have to take the laboratory into the field to study the natural foods of the animals—to China to study food sources for pandas, to Africa to compare the level of vitamin E in grasses from different areas where

Visitors watch the weekly feeding of a bushmaster snake at the Audubon Zoo in New Orleans.

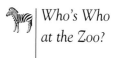
rhinos live or to study the food preferences of marmosets.

Rarely can a zoo duplicate exactly what the animal eats in the wild, but by understanding the nutrients in the diet, a zoo can approximate the quantity and quality.

Nutritionists also need to understand what happens to different nutrients under different conditions—like freezing or drying a food. One might think that giving the rhino hay is fine, since it is dried grass, and grass has plenty of vitamin E. But the process of drying grass, which makes hay, causes it to lose ninety percent of its vitamin E. So either the rhino needs fresh grass or something else with the right amount of the vitamin.

Zoo nutritionists spend a great deal of time in the laboratory analyzing the food and directing quality control on every new shipment of fish, hay or fruit which comes into the commissary where all food is stored. They design diet sheets for the keepers to keep track of what the animals eat every day so that sickness may be traced to a food.

Much of what nutritionists are doing now is basic research, figuring out what animals need to be healthy. Recently, several of the big animal-food companies have developed exotic animal food in addition to the chow we feed our pets.

SAMPLE DIETS
(Courtesy "Animal Fare" column, *Zoolife* magazine, by Jeffrey Burbank)

ANTEATER CHOW IN L.A.

1 lb. commercial bird-of-prey diet (a meat protein mix)
1 scoop of dog chow
2 tbs. yogurt
2 peeled oranges
1 peeled avocado—no seed
1 lb. cottage cheese
Blend well and serve.

MEAT LOAF FOR THE BIRDS
Cleveland Metro Park Zoo

3 scoops game-bird chow
1 box high-protein baby cereal
3 tbs. vitamin E (powdered vitamin)
8 lbs. ground carrots
30 hard-boiled eggs
7 lbs. cooked beef and beef heart
Mix ingredients and serve. Toss in some mealworms and crickets for hunt-and-peck appetizers, and provide fresh fruit for dessert. Serves a flock of insectivorous birds.

SERPENT SLUMGULLION
Oklahoma City Zoo

King cobras only eat other snakes. They have little appetite for mice, the staple for zoo snakes. But since no zoo wants to keep other snakes on the ready for the cobra's dinner, other solutions had to be found. This one is a sauce for the mice. By coating the mice in "snake sauce," the cobras get used to the mice and eventually will eat them without the sauce.
6-8 medium-size snakes (such as rattlesnakes)
1 gallon water
live mice or "pinkies"
Clean the snakes, slice and boil down until the mixture becomes a "soup." Let cool. Dip mice in soup and serve immediately. The soup may be stored for future use.

Animal behavior is very important when it comes to feeding. For example, browsers, those that reach up into the trees for branches, will not eat properly if forced to get their food from the ground. In zoos, food bins are installed high up for giraffes to reach their browse as they would in the wild.

Underwater eaters, like turtles, must have their food put into an edible casing, like sausage, so that the vitamin powders do not wash away. Although it is easier to feed large cats canned foods, studies indicate that nature does know best: eating and chewing on bones, hair and skin or "real" meat keeps them much healthier. In addition, giving them real meat allows them to perform their natural behavior of dragging and playing with the food.

It is crucial that zoo animals eat what is right for them. Visitors must never throw a hot dog, pennies, paper, cigarettes or anything into an animal's enclosure, because they may eat it. Sea lions have been known to swallow plastic bags in zoo pools as well as in the ocean, and that can kill them.

COMMISSARY

The commissary is where the food is stored. Tons of food are delivered every day.

A mini zoo with ten animals (no bird or reptile), would have to stock all the following items each day. Imagine this times 360. That is approximately what it takes to feed the 3,608 animals at the Bronx Zoo/Wildlife Conservation Park.

800 pounds of alfalfa and timothy hay
16 quarts of ground grain (with minerals and salt added)
25 loaves of bread
10 cabbages
4 quarts of crushed oats
25 pounds of raw white potatoes (some whole and unpeeled, some whole and peeled and some diced or chopped)
30 pounds of apples and carrots (some whole, some sliced and some chopped)
12 pounds of pellets made from various grains, minerals and vitamins
12 ounces of Cream of Wheat
1 quart of white milk
1 quart of malted milk
5 cans of evaporated milk
1/2 cup of honey
1/2 quart of corn oil
1/2 pint of cod-liver oil
1 quart of ground-up fish

Commissary at Zoo Atlanta. Large volumes of food have to be prepared every day.

40 pounds of mackerel (whole)
20 pounds of other fish (butterfish, etc.)
  (whole)
6 raw eggs
1 hard-boiled egg
3 slices of Zwieback with currant jelly
1 pint of Jell-O
6 stalks of celery
1 head of lettuce
1 handful of grapes
1 quart of weak tea (with raw eggs in it)
10 cookies or wafers
5 ounces of canned dog food
1 whole orange
8 ounces of sliced peaches with pineapple
  and strawberries
5 sliced plums or apricots
2 bananas
1 cup of diced fresh mixed vegetables and
  greens
1 cup of diced fruit
30 pounds of raw meat (with bone meal
  and cod-liver oil added)
eucalyptus leaves (fresh, mature leaves
  only)
salt block with iodine
multiple vitamin concentrate in
  sweetened orange juice

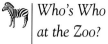
DIRECTOR

The director leads the zoo, makes the major decisions and usually represents the zoo to the public. It was directors like William Hornaday at the Wildlife Conservation Society who had the vision necessary to establish an agenda for zoos throughout the United States. And it is current directors like William Conway who will lead zoos into the twenty-first century.

Directors must deal with the daily tasks of running their zoo, but they must also see beyond the fences to the big picture of the earth and its inhabitants. If zoos are to continue on their evolutionary path, taking an active role in global conservation, then the director must be able to understand environmental problems and use the zoo to find solutions.

Early in American zoo history, the director could be anyone who took an interest in animals. Now, most directors have a scientific background in zoology, ornithology or veterinary medicine. But some come to the zoo with training in business, architecture or wildlife management. Still others become directors by working their way up through the zoo world.

Kevin J. Bell
Lincoln Park Zoo

Kevin Bell grew up following his father around as he tended to his charges. The family even lived where his father worked, the Bronx Zoo/Wildlife Conservation Park, where he directed the bird department for twenty-five years. As a boy, Dr. Bell knew every nook and cranny in the zoo and enjoyed showing his friends around the place he called home. In fact, newspapers called him the boy with 2,830 pets.

Not surprisingly, Kevin Bell eventually got a degree in zoology.

At twenty-three, he became the youngest curator ever hired at the Lincoln Park Zoo. For seventeen years, he has overseen the renovation and construction of several buildings. His international conservation work has helped assure that the number of the endangered Bali mynah has grown from less than twenty birds in the wild to more than fifty.

At the age of forty, he was named the seventh director in the 125-year history of the Lincoln Park Zoo.

William Conway
Wildlife Conservation Society

Since the age of four, Dr. William Conway wanted to be a zookeeper. By the age of twelve, he was out in the field hunting snakes with the reptile curator from the St. Louis Zoo. Even before he graduated from college, he was running the bird department. He came to the Bronx Zoo/Wildlife Conservation Park at the age of twenty-seven and became director six years later. Four years after that he became general director of the Wildlife Conservation Society.

Under his leadership, the Society is a front-runner in exhibit design, breeding and management of species and restoration ecology (improving damaged ecosystems) worldwide. In addition to overseeing all the work of the Society in America and globally, he has written more than two hundred articles and works actively on committees at home and internationally to promote the cause of wildlife. He is as comfortable doing fieldwork on the beaches

Top: Dr. Kevin Bell, Director, Lincoln Park Zoo.

Middle: Dr. William Conway, General Director, Wildlife Conservation Society.

Bottom: Ron Forman, Director of the Audubon Institute.

of Patagonia in Argentina as he is dining formally in some of America's most gracious homes with members of his board of directors or bumping over the African savanna in a jeep.

Ron Forman
The Audubon Institute

As a boy, all the polar bears he ever saw at the zoo were green. Ron Forman thought that was their natural color. The bears swam in pools filled with green algae that coated them. At the time, he did not know that his work as an adult would help correct that situation.

After receiving his master's degree in business administration, he went to work for city government in New Orleans, becoming the liaison to the zoo. Soon thereafter he was appointed director. In 1977, Ron Forman took over what the *New York Times* called "an animal ghetto" and has turned it into a great zoo. He used his business background to create and follow a long-range plan to completely overhaul the facility. Now, as part of the Audubon Institute, a collection of museums in New Orleans dedicated to the natural sciences, the Audubon Zoo has become a showplace for animal care and conservation.

David Hancocks
Arizona–Sonora Desert Museum

David Hancocks was born in England and attended the University of Bath to earn his degree in architecture with honors. He developed an interest in animal architecture (the homes animals build for themselves) and translated that into a concern for the way animals were housed in zoos.

He became director of a wildlife park in England and then moved to Seattle, where he became director of the Woodland Park Zoo. An understanding of animal behavior guided the rebuilding of the zoo. Together with landscape architects Jonquil Jones, Grant Jones and Jon Coe, he created immersion exhibits never before thought possible. After nine years as director at the Woodland Park Zoo, he went to Australia to design several facilities in Perth and Melbourne, then did the

Top: David Hancocks, Director, Arizona–Sonora Desert Museum.

Bottom: Palmer E. Krantz III, Director, Riverbanks Zoological Park.

same in Singapore. Now, he has returned to become director of the Arizona-Sonora Desert Museum.

Palmer E. Krantz III
Riverbanks Zoological Park

"Satch," as Krantz likes to be called, grew up in South Carolina, where he never visited a zoo—none was within easy reach of his home. Yet, he was interested in animals and majored in zoology in college but with no particular aim in mind.

Just before graduating from Clemson University, he read a newspaper account of a zoo that was being built near his home and drove out to take a look. In a pine forest staked

out to become a zoo, he bumped into the man who was director. It was a pivotal conversation. The two spoke for several hours, and the director offered him a job after graduation.

For sixteen months, Satch Krantz drove a tractor, worked in horticulture, set up the animal hospital and learned how to build a zoo from the ground up. In the spring of 1975, he became general curator, and in April of 1976, he became acting director. Four months later he was named director.

He recently celebrated twenty years at the Riverbanks Zoo. Today, the zoo is the most visited attraction in the state, home to 483 species, with expansive education and conservation programs.

Terry Maple
Zoo Atlanta

Dr. Terry Maple has been a psychology professor at a university, has written nearly one hundred scientific papers and is perhaps the world's foremost authority on the great apes—gorillas, orangutans and chimpanzees.

He has studied great apes in the laboratory, in the zoo and in the wild. His knowledge of psychobiology, the interrelationship between psychology and biology (Ph.D. from the University of California), has contributed to his success as a director.

His sensitivity to animals in his care is illustrated by the exceptional gorilla habitat recently completed at the Zoo Atlanta. In their new exhibit, the gorillas live in surroundings as similar as possible to their African homeland. Dr. Maple saw to it that a gorilla named Willy B., who had been kept in a small, indoor cage for nearly twenty years, was able to take his first steps outside into a grassy exhibit and now can opt to be inside or out. He currently lives with two female gorillas and has become a father.

"The worst zoo in the country" is how the Zoo Atlanta was rated by *Parade* magazine nine years ago, when Dr. Maple was named acting director by Mayor Andrew Young. Today, it may well be rated one of the world's finest and has won awards for its innovative exhibits and management.

Top: Dr. Terry Maple, Director, Zoo Atlanta.

Bottom: Thomas C. Otten, Director, Point Defiance Zoo.

Thomas C. Otten
Point Defiance Zoo

Tom Otten began his career as a marine-mammal trainer at Marineland, California, in 1969. He quickly became director of training and used his position to make the shows more educational and to combine the animal-care and training staffs. In this way, visitors had a more involved staff informing them about the marine animals.

As director, he leads one of the country's ten best zoos. In addition to his work in the zoo, he is active in conservation efforts, including bringing the red wolf back from the edge of extinction and the rehabilitation of many marine mammals.

George Rabb
Brookfield Zoo

Dr. George Rabb, a historian and man of great vision, manages a highly respected zoo and zoological society while actively participating in worldwide conservation. At the Brookfield Zoo, where he has been director since 1976, he and his staff have created outstanding educational exhibits. They assure that research in the wild and in the zoo are part of the basic function of the Brookfield Zoo, with projects sponsored around the world.

In addition to his leadership in the zoo world, his research and writings, he is chairman of the Species Survival Commission of the International Union for the Conservation of Nature (IUCN), an organization of great importance to world conservation. Dr. Rabb is able to put where we are today in context with where we have been and plan for where we are going.

Y. Sherry Sheng
Metro Washington Park Zoo

Since she was a little girl in Taiwan, Y. Sherry Sheng has been fascinated by all life forms, from apple seeds to whales. With a degree in zoology and fisheries biology from college in Taiwan, she traveled to the University of Washington in Seattle to study toward a Ph.D. degree.

She spent her few free hours as a guide at the recently opened Seattle Aquarium. Soon she began to teach in their education programs and was named director in 1985. She was chosen director of the Metro Washington Park Zoo in 1988.

Today, the zoo designs exhibits with help from visitors of all ages (including children in elementary groups), boasts an exciting environmental enrichment program that challenges zoo animals to actively explore their space and offers events that showcase the zoo each season (ZooLights in winter, ZooBloom in spring, concerts in summer, ZooBoo in fall).

Below: Dr. George Rabb, Director, Brookfield Zoo.

Bottom: Dr. Y. Sherry Sheng, Director, Metro Washington Park Zoo.

Patricia Simmons
Akron Zoo

Pat Simmons grew up in a town so small the cows outnumbered the people. Zanesfield, Ohio, had four roads, one gas station and about two hundred people. A big draw was the trout hatchery and the all-male fishing club her grandfather had established. Pat Simmons wanted nothing more than to run that hatchery, but it was more acceptable to her family that she follow her other interests and become an art teacher.

She found that teaching art was okay, but through a job in a museum, she found that non-profit institutions serving the community were a more exciting and rewarding environment for her.

At twenty-five, she went with her husband to Akron, where she took a job as a fund-raiser at the failing Akron Zoo, a tiny zoo in a downtrodden part of town. Ms. Simmons saw in it a chance to rebuild something for the community, in a natural setting that pleasantly reminded her of childhood. She also earned a master's degree in business administration.

Patricia Simmons,
Director, Akron Zoo.

In 1985, she was named director and took on the monumental job of improving the zoo so it could be accredited by the AZA. With a small staff and budget, she worked tirelessly. Only four years later, in 1989, the zoo was accredited, membership increased and exhibits were developed to focus the attention of visitors on the need for conservation and protection of wildlife.

CURATOR

Every department in the zoo has a curator. While the keepers take care of the animals directly, the curator is responsible for all the keepers in the department as well as the animals. Curators decide with others what animals are going to breed, what animals should be traded to other zoos and what animals the zoo needs to strengthen its own collection. Curators typically have higher college degrees, including Ph.D.s, in their area of expertise. An individual will have years of academic training as well as years of hands-on experience before becoming a curator.

HORTICULTURIST AND LANDSCAPE ARCHITECT

As zoos strive to create more naturalistic exhibits, the need for a diverse plant life becomes more and more important to replicate the ecosystem the animals naturally live in. The plantings also make the visitor feel as though he is immersed in the environment. Creating this setting is where the horticulturist comes in.

The Arizona-Sonora Desert Museum has 1,200 species of plant on display. The Leid Jungle at the Henry Doorly Zoo in Omaha, Nebraska, has three thousand species of plant, including twenty-five species of bamboo. In order to grow strong trunks, trees require wind to sway them. Without any natural wind in the building, the Leid Jungle has human tree shakers. The Metro Toronto Zoo planted 20,000 trees and shrubs as background to their exhibits. The horticulturist is integral in planning the exhibits, choosing plants which are found in the natural habitat of the animal or similar ones. They must plan for the right containers, soil, light, drainage and maintenance of the plants that will go into the exhibit. They must know what plants are indestructible or will be left alone by the animals because they have spikes or a bad taste. And they must know what plants might be poisonous to the animals.

Landscape architects design with plants, providing natural-looking environments. They must anticipate what the vegetation will look like after years of growth—how high, wide and dense they will become. There are now computer programs which help them envision the physical changes of plantings over time.

RESEARCHER AND RESEARCH COORDINATOR

The position of research coordinator is a fairly new one in some zoos. But since zoos have become the only places where animals can be studied in a seminatural state or the only places where some animals can survive, they have become key places for research. Students studying biology, psychology or ethology observe zoo animals. Research in zoos can be productive because one can observe animals close up, carry out comparative studies knowing the family history of the animals and control situations more easily than one can in the wild. The research coordinator organizes the schedules and maintains an overview of all the research.

Researchers study animals in the zoo because they are not able to get to the wild. They also want to gain a better understanding of how animals live in captivity. Several projects may be going on at the same time: one researcher observing maternal behavior in baboons, another analyzing primate vocalizations, someone else studying the problem of ovulation in black rhinos.

Much of the important research done in zoos is done by students. It is through such work that much has been learned about reproduction, enrichment and basic behavior.

An imaginative example of how research in zoos and in the wild can be combined is illustrated by a program called ChimpanZoo. For more than thirty years, Dr. Jane Goodall has studied chimpanzees in the wild, in the Gombe National Park in Tanzania. No one in the world knows chimp behavior better than Dr. Goodall.

Life is perilous for wild chimpanzees, with

Jon Coe is a landscape architect by training who now concentrates mostly on zoo exhibit design. Using his knowledge of ecology, space, psychology (human and animal) and plantings, he has created some of the cutting-edge exhibits in the United States today. Jon will travel to the animals' natural habitat to observe their interaction with the ecosystem in order to re-create the best possible environment for them in the zoo.

habitat and numbers threatened. It became clear to Dr. Goodall that, while continuing research in the wild, it was also important to assure the best possible care for the 1,200 chimpanzees in captivity in North America. A large part of that population are zoo animals.

Basic zoo chimp behavior had to be observed and compared to wild behavior. How were zoo chimps similar, how were they different? How did zoo chimps respond to their caging? Currently, the study includes 150 chimps in fifteen zoos.

During a sixteen-week training program, observers learn to recognize approximately fifty categories of behavior. All the data are standardized and fed into a computer, with the goal of acquiring a better understanding of how captive animals adjust to captivity. These many observers involve themselves in the lives of the animals. In addition to collecting information they also often enrich and improve conditions for the captive chimps.

ARCHIVIST, PHOTOGRAPHER AND ARTIST

Not all zoos can afford to have a graphics department, so they hire outside artists to create signs, pamphlets, maps, even invitations to zoo events. Many big zoos do have a graphics department, a photo archive, a publications department and a library.

In the graphics department, artists plan the design of everything from the brochure a visitor receives at the gate to signs at exhibits. The descriptive signs around the exhibits have to be written and illustrated in the same style to avoid confusion. Throughout the zoo, there are signs offering information about the animals and the exhibits and signs that give direction. Often the signs set a mood. For example, all the signs may look rustic in an African exhibit area; in the children's zoo they may be playful. Most zoo signs also use icons. The standard simple signs that everyone will understand include DO NOT FEED THE ANIMALS. Most zoos have added a new one that means THIS IS AN ENDANGERED ANIMAL. It looks like a rhino and a baby rhino.

All the animals in the zoo collection are photographed. Most zoos have a photographer on call to take pictures of the animals and to record births and special events.

The photo archive is a library of photographs, a place to maintain a record of the animals in the collection. Often, people writing books or articles may use these photos from the archives.

The zoo photographer may also set up TV cameras which offer the public a view into the private living quarters of the animals. For most species, following a birth, it is best to leave the mother and baby alone. The stress of visitors may cause the mother to reject the baby. The risk of infection is also high if people have close contact. Yet, a camera can record what is going on between mother and baby in the den and project it out to the public area. This protects the animals while allowing the visitor to be a part of the scene. In the Central Park Wildlife Center, a tiny camera in the colony of leaf-cutter ants takes people where they otherwise could never go—down into the trails and caverns made by the ants.

The library, like the photo archive, is a place of reference for zoo staff and public, stocked with scientific magazines, papers and books—some written by the people who work in the zoo.

The library can also be a historical archive, containing letters, old zoo guides, magazine articles and even animal medical records passed from one generation to another.

PUBLIC AFFAIRS

This department is where fund-raising is focused and material is produced about the zoo to inform the public.

Typically, zoos will have signs thanking companies and individuals for making contributions. Some zoos have animal-adoption programs—for a certain amount of money every year, one can "adopt" an elephant or naked mole rat.

The public relations department gets stories into the newspaper, on TV or on the radio. If something happens at the zoo that people want to know about, like the death of an animal or the long-awaited birth of an elephant, public relations people must be ready to talk with reporters or to arrange for the zoo director to hold a press conference.

Joan Embry

Perhaps the best known spokesperson for a zoo is Joan Embry, goodwill ambassador for the San Diego Zoological Society. For twenty-five years she has raised, trained and talked about more animals than she can possibly recall.

Joan was considering a career as a veterinarian and thought that some experience at a zoo would help. She started working at the San Diego Zoo in 1968 as a Children's Zoo attendant. That is where she gave a young Asian elephant material to paint with. The painting elephant put them both on the Johnny Carson show for the first time, something she was to repeat over seventy-five times with a variety of animals. In addition, she has appeared on other shows, at zoos, conservation organizations, schools, on the radio and even on cruise ships—always to introduce her audience to the wonders of the animals she brings with her. Joan estimates that over a billion people have seen her on television. She gets fan mail from all over the globe.

Joan Embry knows her animals. She is very experienced in the care of many species and continues to work with them today. Her knowledge, her calm and her good humor have made it possible for her to bring delight and information to a huge audience. Always prepared for the unpredictable, she has taken every imaginable creature before television cameras. Whether amidst the cute antics (Johnny Carson had a marmoset pee on his head) or keeping rhinos calm, Joan's message is one of conservation and care for animals.

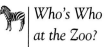

Joan Embry and "Kler," a female spotted cuscus native to New Guinea.

Section III
Looking to the Future

Chapter Six
ON THE EDGE OF EXTINCTION

S cientists from various disciplines disagree about many things, but about the urgency to save species and the biological health of the planet, they speak as one: The next fifty years are critical.

We are only beginning to realize the diversity of life on earth. Scientists have identified 1.2 million species on the planet, yet they believe that species still undiscovered in rain forest canopies, soils, the ocean floor and other poorly understood ecosystems

may bring the number to as high as 100 million.

There are thirty species of mite living in the feathers of a Mexican parrot. There can be as many as forty-three species of ant living in one tree. As recently as the 1990s, primate species were being discovered. At the same time, half of the 225 identified primate species are threatened with extinction. There are few places where wildlife is safe. Only 3.7 percent of the earth is protected land. The rest is being overrun with the human species. And still the human population continues to grow, perhaps doubling to ten billion by the year 2000. Most of this growth is occurring in the poorer countries, where a majority of the earth's remaining wild areas are concentrated.

The result of this overpopulation is that humans have destroyed the balance of most wildlife populations. Ecosystems have been destroyed as people cut down forests, cultivated prairies, built dams and polluted waters. Plants die and animals are overhunted. Plants and animals have evolved to live in specific niches. If their habitats are destroyed, so are they. If a settlement or highway is built in the path of a migratory route, the animals will persist in trying to use that established path; it is programmed into their behavior. The migrating animals will collide with the human construction and the animals will always lose.

Dr. E. O. Wilson, a biologist at Harvard University, estimates that twenty-seven thousand species per year—seventy-four per day, or three per hour—are becoming extinct. They will be gone and cannot be brought back. Dr. Wilson estimates that at this rate, twenty

The graveyard at the Bronx Zoo/Wildlife Conservation Park is erected every Earth Day. Each tombstone represents one species of animal that has recently become extinct or is endangered.

percent of the earth's species will be extinct in thirty years.

This terrible imposition on so many other species is upsetting the critical balance in the web of life. All life is interrelated and dependent on other life. The elimination of one or two or fifty species will have effects that we cannot predict. Extinctions are creating change even before we understand the consequences.

Some people see no reason for the fuss about protecting the environment since over the known history of life on earth there have been five mass extinctions. The last was sixty-five million years ago, when the dinosaurs became extinct along with many other forms of life. It took twenty million years for the diversity of species to recover after that crisis. What is different about this extinction spasm? It is happening so fast, and humans are the cause.

Humans are destroying rain forests (as much as two football fields every second) and oceans.

We are causing desertification, erosion, pollution and ozone depletion.

Mass extinctions, like the one that killed off the dinosaurs, may well have been caused by natural disasters, but we know that more contemporary extinctions are because of human behavior: over-population, over-hunting and over-development of land. By over-hunting, our ancestors contributed to the extinction of the mastodon, more recently the dodo (a big flightless bird extinct by 1681) and the passenger pigeon (by the end of the 1800s).

Even when habitats remain, they can become fragmented, separated by roads or towns to become little islands. Fragmentation keeps animals of the same species apart, with severe consequences. Animals living in these little pockets cannot get together to mate. Animals in the same fragmented habitat develop habits of inbreeding, which can destroy a species.

Other humans are trying to protect wildlife,

Human overpopulation has destroyed the balance of most wildlife populations. Ecosystems have been destroyed as people cut down forests, cultivated prairies, built dams and polluted waters. Plants die and animals are overhunted.

and now there is a growing awareness that a fur coat is more beautiful on a large cat than on a woman, that wolves and wood bison and snail darters also have a place on the earth and that not only can humans co-exist with them, but the worldwide ecosystem needs them.

Positive change is beginning to replace negative change on a global scale. The Earth Summit in Brazil during the summer of 1992 was an important moment for global change. Governments of the world worked together as though they actually lived on the same earth. Yet, action is still slow.

There are many organizations working on the issues that face the earth, including the United Nations Environmental Program (UNEP), the International Union for the Conservation of Nature (IUCN), the World Conservation Monitoring Center (WCMC), the World Wildlife Fund (WWF), the National Association of Environmental Educators (NAEE), the Humane Society of the United States (HSUS), which has opened an international division, and the United Nations Children's Relief Fund (UNICEF), which has started an environmental division.

Zoos have an overview of the world's animals and ecosystems. Zoo professionals are making provisions for the future. One way is to protect "keystone" species. Currently these large mammals, carnivores (tigers, jaguars) and herbivores (elephants, rhinos), are dangerously threatened with extinction. Keystone species help form and keep together ecosystems. Since they require large habitats to survive, they also help support much of other plant and animal life. They are part of a diverse food chain. If elephants are hunted to

Wildlife biologist Ian Douglas Hamilton and others examine corpse of poached elephant.

extinction, there will be consequences for the other animals that have evolved to live alongside the elephants. The elephants become the representatives for their habitats—the "keystone."

The creative and adaptive mind of humans can make change. The condition of the planet can change. The earth can come into balance again. People working in zoos today may not be alive when the day comes, but someday habitats may once again be safe and the animals may then be able to return to their natural homes.

Left: Daggers made of rhino horns on display.

Bottom: Confiscated ivory warehouse.

Rondonia , Brazil—Once nearly 8 million square miles of rain forest encircled the equatorial region of the globe, today, well over half of it has been destroyed. The rain forest continues to be cut and burned at an alarming rate. The clearcutting of the rain forest for farmland, roads and timber destroys more than the trees. The other plants , animals and human cultures who are dependent on that habitat also face extinction.

Chapter Seven
ONTO THE LIFE RAFT

Through the expert efforts of many zoos, species otherwise doomed to extinction are surviving, and may be returned to the wild someday. To assure physically and genetically healthy animals for future generations, there must be a scientifically tested breeding program for each species. The AZA (American Zoo and Aquarium Association) has developed a North American breeding and conservation program, called the Species Survival Plan (SSP), a

critical part of what zoos are doing to assure the survival of species in their care. They are an insurance policy against extinction. One of the primary goals of the SSP is to attempt to save carefully selected species through captive breeding, habitat preservation and supportive research. It is the hope that some of these animals may be returned to the wild; however, maintaining genetic variation within a species, important scientific research and educating the public are all important goals within the Species Survival Plan.

It is the SSP which may allow our great-grandchildren's grandchildren to see a snow leopard like the one in the zoo and the one that still roams high in the desolate Himalayan mountains.

The combination of healthy animal popu-lations managed through SSPs, preservation of natural habitat, reintroductions, increased scientific knowledge and public awareness will hopefully result in a brighter future for many of today's endangered species.

Animals and plants are able to adapt and evolve with great diversity because of information stored in their genes. It is these tiny bits of information strung together in chromosomes that cause plants, animals and humans to be both the same and different.

Menageries did not plan or manage the breeding of animals. Most had only one animal from a particular species on display. If animals of the same species did mate, there was no thought to the genetic composition of the offspring or planning for how the captive animals would survive into future generations.

If the same population of animals and their offspring mate repeatedly among themselves, then the limited combination of genes can result in "inbreeding." If groups of animals never get any new genetic material into their population, because individuals from the same "family" breed again and again, there is greater likelihood of illness, deformities and sterility.

In nature, most species have behaviors that prevent this from happening. In many species, the individual animals gather together in large groups at breeding grounds during the mating season. This assures a broad range of individuals to choose from. Solitary animals come together to mate and then part again. Male and female snow leopards live in their own territories, find each other only to mate, assuring the next generation, and then go on their way. Social animals like chimpanzees have very close relationships with their mothers, brothers and sisters, but the males seek unrelated females from another group as their mates.

In zoos, sometimes animals breed that are genetically similar but not of the same species. For example, two members of the cat family, lion and tiger, have been intentionally bred to produce odd mixes still on display in some present-day menageries: ligers. Even in accredited zoos, as recently as the past decade, subspecies such as the rare Sumatran and Bornean orangutans mated and produced offspring. Although there may be nothing wrong with crossbreeding of closely related species (it does occur in nature), it must be done with forethought and planning to preserve the health of animal populations and the genetic variability of the species. The SSP is trying to maintain the potential for future evolution. Natural selection cannot act in the absence of genetic variation and when a population loses genetic variation it is less able to respond to changing environmental conditions.

If future generations are to be returned to the wild, then it is critical that we maintain a healthy breeding population. We don't know what future human generations will be able to do to protect wildlife. We want to leave them a broad representation of endangered species.

Until the present crisis of extinction, not much attention was paid to keeping subspecies pure. We are not conscious of preserving the differences that nature took millions of years to develop. We don't know what impact we may be having by stirring the pot, by mixing genes. Geneticists have become critical members of the zoo team. Many work directly in zoos and others from universities collaborate with zoo professionals.

PLANNING FOR SPECIES SURVIVAL

For many years top zoo professionals recognized the need for a detailed census of animals in zoos. In 1973, Dr. Ulysses Seal and Dale Makey proposed the International Species Inventory System (ISIS) in an effort to survey all the animals held in captivity at the time and with anticipation of the conservation problems in the future. In 1974, with funding from AZA, AAZV and other sources including the U.S. Department of the Interior, ISIS became a reality.

Today, ISIS, based at the Minnesota Zoological Garden and under the directorship of biologist Nate Flesness, is a computer system that links information on captive animals and their ancestors in the world's participating zoos in thirty-nine countries. ISIS is well on its way to enabling zoos to have an overview of the demographics of captive animals worldwide.

One software package developed by ISIS, ARKS (Animal Records Keeping System), is used in 350 facilities worldwide to collect and distribute accurate and detailed records on individual animals when and if the zoo provides the information.

MedARKS (Medical Animal Records Keeping System), standardizes medical information, including anesthesia records, parasitology exams, drug treatment and vaccinations. It allows veterinarians in zoos to benefit by

Lowland gorilla Jessica with baby Mike at the San Diego Zoo. Under the SSP, lowland gorillas are breeding very successfully in captivity.

accessing information they currently do not have for a species or individual animal. And SPARKS (Single Population Analysis and Record Keeping System) was developed by ISIS and the AZA's Small Population Management Advisory Group (SPMAG) to assist the production of studbooks using genetic and demographic analyses for the entire captive population of any species.

ISIS is the only global database available. Of course, it can only include information if the institutions who have the animals take the time to provide it to ISIS. At this time, the survival of a species may depend on the careful selection of a mate based on the genetics of the animals. Mates are selected on the basis of "mean kinship," a measure of how related an individual animal is to all other individuals in the population. The less closely related they are the more genetic variability their offspring will have, contributing to the health of the population.

The Species Survival Plan

In 1979, a report played an influential role in motivating the zoo world to chart a new direction. Although for decades geneticists had developed the theory that inbreeding in a population was detrimental, Katherine Ralls, a research scientist at the National Zoo, demonstrated using a computer model that if no changes were made it was possible that zoo animals would become so inbred that they could not sustain healthy populations. It was even possible that captive animal populations would die out within 150 years.

Curators and zoo directors took notice. The American Zoo and Aquarium Association (AZA) became the clearing house to sort out the "gene pool" problem. The gene pool refers to all the genes available for a single population of animals. As wild populations get smaller and destroyed habitat leaves little territory for the animals to roam, the gene pool diminishes. Managing a diminished gene pool for variability, viability and compatibility is a rigorous science.

At the moment there are approximately six hundred snow leopards in captivity. If those animals have the same grandparents or parents, as often happens in small captive populations, then the gene pool becomes smaller. There is less variability and more unhealthy offspring.

The AZA created the Species Survival Plan (SSP) to keep species healthy and prevent Dr. Ralls's prediction. The SSP is a detailed plan outlining which animals within a certain species population should breed, when, how often and with what individuals. The plan projects management to meet the goals of each program whether that is a long-

Snow leopards naturally live in the highlands of central Asia, in a rough and barren landscape. Because prey is scarce, each snow leopard needs a great deal of territory to survive. The harsh environment and the people who inhabit the area have endangered the snow leopard. The cats are hunted for their beautiful coats. One coat is worth a year's wages to a local family who have barely enough food to survive. It is unlikely that the land will ever be safe for them to be returned to the wild. But, if that day comes, there will be genetically strong animals to be reintroduced. The captive breeding programs are not the solution to saving species, but they are leaving open a window of opportunity. They can also help raise public awareness of and funds in support of field conservation efforts.

Siberian tiger mother with cubs. It is important to keep a healthy captive population, yet currently there is room for only 1,000 Siberian tigers in world zoos. The current population is at capacity. The SSP must maintain a healthy genetically diverse number without overpopulation.

term breeding plan for reintroduction or to increase the wild population. The goal of some of the SSP programs is to breed animals quickly and return them immediately to the wild. Dr. Conway calls this CPR or captive propagation rescue.

The first step before SSPs could be created was to determine what species each zoo was exhibiting and which zoos had the same species. In many cases, the animals were consolidated to assure the healthiest population. The creation of the SSP program marked the beginning of a change in attitude within the zoo community from competition to cooperation for the preservation of species.

A rule of animal management is never to concentrate all the members of a species in one place, so that if one group gets sick or suffers some cataclysm, at least another group untouched by the calamity has a good chance of surviving. Working with ISIS, zoos began

a coordinated survey of all animals in captivity: age, sex, history (where it came from, born in the wild or in a zoo, which zoo), genealogy, health history, and individual characteristics. The SSP, while not very romantic, assures that a good match is made which will produce the healthiest possible animals of the species for at least two hundred years.

Because most wild populations of animals are threatened and there are now laws to protect them, no new animals are captured from the wild except in extreme circumstances when there is just not enough diversity in the gene pool to keep the species healthy. Almost all zoo animals are born to parents already in zoos (ninety-two percent of all new mammals, seventy percent of birds).

Founder animals are unrelated individuals on which a captive population is established. Although typically captured from the wild, founders can be captive born but unrelated to animals presently in the SSP population. The more founder animals in the captive population, the better for the species. Founder animals provide a greater mix of genes because they are assumed to be unrelated.

There are many animals in the world needing protection and only a limited number of those are in zoos. Currently, 5,743 vertebrate species are held in zoos worldwide, many at risk. Deciding which are to be a part of the SSP program is difficult. Geneticists, biologists, zoo directors, curators and ecologists ponder those decisions.

Currently the AZA's Conservation and Science Office, under the leadership of Dr. Michael Hutchins, has responsibility for coordinating and facilitating programs and information throughout the worldwide network of concerned conservationists. The AZA believes that as well as establishing captive breeding programs, efforts must also be focused on field conservation. Even before establishing an SSP, consideration must be given to whether it will contribute to preserving the species or ecosystem in nature.

Currently there are sixty-two SSPs in North American zoos, representing one hundred and eight species including: forty-nine mammals, fifteen birds, six reptiles and amphibians, thirty-four freshwater fish and four invertebrates.

There are, of course, many more species which could benefit from management through SSPs. Some professionals feel the number of SSPs should be much greater, even as many as 2,000. There are no clear-cut answers to many of the important issues and decisions. The AZA points out that resources are very limited, and the SSPs are only one critical link in the overall effort to preserve species and the ecosystems they inhabit. Time, space and money must be carefully targeted for the most important "flagship" species, which have the ability to excite public attention and thus contribute to broader conservation goals for all species and habitat preservation.

Studbook Keeper

The studbook documents all the information about each individual of each species. Back in the 1950s, zoo directors, as good managers and thinking ahead of the extinction crisis, were keeping detailed records of some species, including Siberian tigers and Przewalski's horses, but there was no consistency for all species. Today there are nearly 200 well-kept studbooks and many more worldwide, with more on the way. The studbook keeper is the key person in charge of maintaining the population database.

AZA Regional Studbooks cover both the United States and Canada. The studbook keeper knows all the individuals of the species within this region; he/she knows the family tree. The information provided by the studbook keeper is then analyzed by the SSP coordinator and management groups. The SSP coordinator and the management groups then make recommendations about what animals should be paired, traded or exchanged to provide the best possible genetic combinations.

Sometimes animals are traded, or sent to another zoo on breeding loan. A male orangutan may "belong" to a zoo in Georgia but be sent to Washington, D.C., to become the father of the National Zoo's female orangutan's babies.

Studbook keepers stay in contact with the curators and keepers participating in the SSPs through animal surveys, generally conducted right after the breeding season. On the average of every three years the individual SSP master plans are reevaluated and updated.

North American SSPs are the leaders in managing captive populations of endangered species. Similar programs are evolving in other regions of the world, including Europe, Australia, and Japan.

Some SSPs have already experienced some exciting successes. The Asian wild horse, the black-footed ferret and the Arabian oryx, while all extinct in the wild, were kept alive

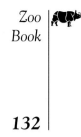
It is estimated only five thousand snow leopards exist in the wild. Of the nearly six hundred snow leopards in captivity worldwide in 1993 only 260 were in the SSP. It is not necessary for the entire captive population to be part of the SSP. It is the job of the studbook keeper to determine the number of animals necessary to maintain a healthy breeding population.

and bred within zoos. The ferret and oryx have since been reintroduced into their natural habitat, with some success. The California condor program is just beginning. There may be as many as twelve SSP species currently involved in reintroduction programs. Unfortunately many captive breeding and reintroduction programs may have begun too late. The endangered species have two strikes against them. Their numbers in the wild are too small and the scientifically based techniques for reintroduction are just beginning to be understood.

SNOW LEOPARD SSP

Few animals are as beautiful or rare as the snow leopard. Thousands of these large cats have been killed for their coats. It is estimated that only five thousand survive in the wild today. There are presently close to six hundred living in fifty zoos around the world.

The snow leopard SSP, started in 1984, is a model for how an organized cooperative breeding program works. Using all the information available from the studbooks, a careful management plan was mapped out to guide the breeding program. At the Bronx Zoo/Wildlife Conservation Park alone, sixty-four cats have been born and have gone to zoos worldwide, contributing to the captive gene pool. By now, Dr. Dan Wharton, Curator, the Wildlife Conservation Society and studbook keeper for the snow leopard, is able to predict how many kittens will be born each year. If properly mixed and matched, there is enough genetic variation to keep the population healthy for many generations.

Most of the snow leopards start breeding in captivity when they are five years old. Eleven years old is the limit of the breeding age. Most of the females have three or four cubs in their lifetimes (the average litter size is two).

When breeding the animals, zoos must consider how much space can be allotted to the species and how much it will cost to keep them throughout their entire lives, not just for the years they are on display or breeding. Numbers of animals have to be controlled because of space limitations, while assuring genetic hardiness.

There are other groups of people who come together to evaluate the world view of

species and habitats. They help assure communication between all organizations (mostly, but not exclusively, zoos) involved in the conservation of animals.

TAGs (Taxon Advisory Groups) work out solutions for whole groups or taxa of animals. They evaluate subspecies and certain individuals with current scientific information, as well as considering ethical issues and animal care techniques.

FIGs (Faunal Interest Groups) are networks of people, both in zoos and in other professions, that plan and work to implement AZA conservation efforts in specific geographical areas of the world. Presently there are FIGs for Madagascar, Southeast Asia, Brazil, Zaire and the West Indies. FIGs are planned for other biologically diverse regions. In 1992-93 alone, AZA and its member institutions supported or initiated over 1,100 scientific and conservation projects in over sixty countries worldwide.

REPRODUCTION IN THE ZOO

Sometimes a male and female are paired in a perfect match. But for some reason, physical or social, they will not mate or do not produce living offspring. Not all animals are willing or able to breed in captivity. Sometimes we know why and sometimes we don't.

Gerenuks are dainty antelope that live on the fringe of the African savanna. In captivity, they just would not breed. Why not? Understanding behavior was the key. In nature, they get all their moisture from the vegetation they feed on. But by having as much water as they wanted in the exhibit, the chemicals by which females signaled readiness to the males became diluted. Once the keepers limited the water to natural levels, the signal was clear and babies were soon born.

Every species requires specific conditions to breed—to be hot, cold, wet, separated from the opposite sex for months before mating, or to have special nesting material. Humans who care for the animals must observe behavior (in the wild, if possible) and provide the right environment.

It becomes even more complicated when animals do not naturally reproduce easily. The giant panda is fertile only for several days of the year. If the female does not become

Female gerenuks.

pregnant, it is a long wait until the next try. We still know so little about both wild and captive animals that it is difficult for even the best medical technology to assure that the animals become pregnant.

Research

Veterinarians and reproductive biologists help nature along through research, which has uncovered some biological secrets. Gene mapping, or DNA fingerprinting, takes a cell sample from blood or skin and turns it into

Dr. Betsy Dresser, head of the Cincinnati Zoo's Center for Reproduction of Endangered Wildlife, placing frozen gametes into the container which holds the frozen zoo.

a map of an individual's genetic composition. This is invaluable if scientists wish to know who the father is, for example, in a group of herd animals when a female may have mated with several males. The procedure provides critical information for SSP breeding recommendations.

For example, a researcher observing a chimpanzee can pick up food the chimpanzee has discarded, put it in alcohol, and send it to the lab. Skin cells from the cheek will have mixed with the food while the chimp chewed. The

technology takes the cell and turns it into the chimp's personal chain of genes, his gene map. All from a single cell, like a fingerprint, it identifies that individual chimp.

Medical technology makes it possible to tell the sex of a bird from a drop of blood. For many species of birds, it is impossible to tell male from female unless one looks inside surgically. With the prick of a needle, curators can be confident they are getting a male and female together, increasing the possibility of offspring.

NEW TECHNOLOGY OF REPRODUCTION

In May of 1984, at the Louisville Zoo, a horse named Kelly gave birth to a zebra. This was no accident, but a result of many years of research. Scientists hope that by perfecting embryo transplants and in vitro fertilization, it will become easier and safer to use domestic animals as mothers for endangered or rare animals. This technique has been used for years to increase the numbers of "prize" livestock born. The egg and sperm of the rare species are combined in the laboratory and the resulting embryos are implanted in host mothers.

The embryos of the endangered animals can be implanted in related domestic animals. In this way, a species with a small population, on the brink of extinction, can grow faster than it would if only the few females of the species were having babies. It also makes it possible to bring new genetic material into a different population without taking the risks of moving an endangered adult animal.

Examples of interspecies embryo transfer are holstein cows giving birth to endangered gaurs, elands to bongos, and domestic cats to the highly endangered Indian desert cat. Of course this is not always possible, even in closely related species.

FROZEN ZOOS

Researchers in zoos are also perfecting the technology of freezing the sperm and embryos. With few exceptions, eggs cannot currently be frozen. Only the sperm can be frozen from animals alive today. If this technique, cryogenics, is perfected, says Dr. Wharton, we can freeze "evolutionary time." These genetically variable animals can be "born" decades or centuries from now, still prepared to return to their natural habitat. There are many limitations to the idea of "frozen zoos," namely behaviors which are "learned" and passed on from generation to generation will be lost. Frozen zoos are an interesting area of exploration but only one part of saving a species.

Condensing essential genetic material like this also frees up some limited space in zoos for other endangered animals. The whole animal does not need to be in the zoo. The genetic material representing the animal can be kept in a small container.

The ability to set up savings banks for genetic material has come from years of research. The technique for freezing elephant semen is different from that for freezing marmoset semen. Testing and trial and error have now made it possible to set up frozen zoos. The future for some species rests in those test tubes. Several zoos in North America now have frozen zoos. For example, the Carl H. Lindner Family Center for Reproduction of Endangered Wildlife (CREW) has developed a "Frozen Zoo and Garden." It is located at the Cincinnati Zoo in Ohio and works closely with the University of Cincinnati College of Medicine to perfect and use frozen genes.

Frozen at −196°C are semen and embryos of dozens of animals, including the snow leopard, white and black rhinos, cheetah and gaur and genes of rare plants. At CREW, the public is able to walk through the building and see every aspect of work at the facility. The visitor can look down onto the work of a technician preparing the material for freezing, or at a monitor which has the magnified image of an embryo-splitting procedure using a needle no larger than a human hair to create twins from a single embryo.

Dr. Betsy Dresser, director of research at CREW, and her colleagues at the Cincinnati Zoo have been making great advances in reproductive research. A recent success was the nonsurgical removal of embryos from a very rare

antelope, the bongo. The bongo embryos were safely flown across the country from Los Angeles and implanted in an eland, with resulting healthy babies. The next step of the project, in cooperation with the Kenyan Wildlife Service in Africa, is to implant bongo embryos in an entire herd of elands, thereby repopulating an area where hunting has killed all the

native bongos. This project could ultimately serve as a model for global embryo exchange.

These techniques have encouraging potential for bringing founder material into the captive population without actually having to take a wild animal from its habitat.

Technology is also helping to provide optimum conditions for successful births in captivity. Biotelemetry, electronically measuring

A bongo calf born to an eland at the Cincinnati Zoo.

activity and temperature from a distance without wires, has helped scientists, in the wild and in the zoos, keep track of animals even when they cannot see them. A computer emits sounds and signals that can be picked up at distance with an antenna or on another computer.

Dr. Christine Sheppard, Curator of Ornithology at the Wildlife Conservation Society, works to conserve many endangered birds. One of her areas of interest is to understand the differences between white-naped and hooded

Artificial egg used in white-naped crane research. The plastic egg encases a transmitter and microprocessor which detects the temperature and humidity of the environment as well as how frequently the parent crane turns the egg in the nest. Ideally, with the information gathered from the artificial egg, conditions could be repeated for the eggs of endangered birds.

cranes, both threatened species. Dr. Sheppard designed a research project to test the conditions necessary for successful artificial incubation—often critical for the eggs to hatch. She needed to understand the climate that surrounds an egg in the nest—how warm, how humid, how often the egg is turned—all things critical for the chick to survive but which humans cannot see.

The goal was to design an egg that could be monitored. Ideally, with the information learned from the artificial egg, similar conditions could be re-created for the real eggs. Although similar work had already been done in the peregrine falcon program with success, the eggs of every species of bird have different requirements.

Working with Dr. Fred Koontz, also of the Wildlife Conservation Society, and electronics expert George Stetten, they were able to design a transmitter and microprocessor (so light it can be glued on a feather) and used a plastic custom-built egg as the casing. Placed in the nest, the fake egg detected the heat and humidity of the environment, and how often it was turned by the crane.

Among the things learned were that the birds turned the eggs every hour and that they cannot control humidity. Therefore, birds native to a very dry climate may not be able to hatch live chicks in a very humid climate, which explained why they do not hatch under artificial conditions. With the kind of information gained by Dr. Sheppard's study optimal conditions may be created for the white-naped cranes and perhaps applied to other endangered birds.

For all the best intentions of the SSPs, and even with a careful breeding plan, there may be erosion, or change of genetic material over time. The focus of research is to assure that, in any event, the best possible genetic representative will still exist for future generations. Everything we are learning about managing captive populations can and will be applied in nature as well. Many species in the wild survive in tiny numbers, limiting genetic material within the population. Animals in the wild face the same crisis as zoo animals. Wildlife preserves and national parks may have to be managed as "megazoos" if they are to survive.

PROBLEMS

One huge problem for zoos is limited space. There may soon be no more room at the zoo. All of the zoos in the United States could fit into the borough of Brooklyn, New York: 88.8 square miles. Not much space for so many zoos. It is estimated that no more than one thousand tigers can live in the zoos of the

White-naped crane.

world. Decisions have to be made to limit the number of births for some animals. Most captive animals have their breeding controlled in some way by contraceptives or sterilization, or by keeping the males and females separated.

Should the zoo euthanize older animals? Yes seems to be the logical answer in many cases. But the public gets very upset to hear that a favorite old tiger must die to make room for new animals. It is a difficult situation, but one that zoos must confront continually.

Another problem arises when a zoo has more animals than it has room for. Zoos must trade or sell animals to other accredited zoos when they do not fit into a breeding program in their zoo. But the reality is that there are sometimes more animals than can be properly cared for anywhere.

There are 1,400 registered animal exhibitors in the United States, and only 162 are AZA-accredited zoos and aquariums. This means that there is potential for a lot of mismanagement of animals. What happens to the surplus animals? They may go to a circus, a game ranch or a menagerie. AZA states that its zoos will place surplus animals in acceptable alternative facilities only. But what are the other non-AZA-accredited institutions doing with their animals? These are tough issues, but not impossible ones. An informed public can press for wise solutions.

Chapter Eight
WILD WORK

We now have a good understanding of reproduction and the genetic requirements of saving a species from extinction. Yet, if there is to be the remotest chance of returning them to a safe, natural habitat, we must understand their life in the wild.

Only after thousands of hours of study and observation of animals can we have some sense of their behavior, what size territory they need, their social and family interactions, predator/prey relationships, health problems, reproduction, nutritional needs and the multitude of other aspects that contribute to a thorough understanding of a species.

How do we get that kind of information? Who are the people spending their lives in jungles, deserts, rain forests, oceans and every conceivable habitat of the planet out of a commitment to knowing another species?

If it were not for the work of wildlife biologists, we would scarcely know anything at all.

Throughout history, people like Charles Darwin and Aristotle have observed and written about animals in their natural habitats. Yet, it is only recently that ethology, the study of the natural behavior of animals, has become a recognized profession. Only during the past thirty years have detailed and systematic data been collected on an international scale. This knowledge has furthered our understanding of many different disciplines involving animals: biology, mammalogy, herpetology, ornithology and ichthyology. The study of ethology also enhances our understanding of other behavioral sciences, such as anthropology, psychology, sociology and even climate studies and earth sciences.

People like Jane Goodall, George Schaller, Dian Fossey, Jonah Western and Alan Rabinowitz have earned great recognition for their research during the past ten to forty years.

In the early 1950s, George Schaller was the first man to produce a long-term study of mountain gorillas. Only then did we learn anything about these incredible great apes. In a human generation, we have come from the first study to a frightening situation where the gorillas may not survive into the next decade.

The men and women who spend so much time in the wild studying animals in their natural surroundings are often unknown. Yet, they are critical to the survival and understanding of the natural world.

These scientists are biologists, ethologists, ecologists or botanists; they must also become politicians and anthropologists in order to be effective in their work in the wild. They have to be creative, learning to make do with scant supplies. They must be linguists, learning other languages in order to communicate with the indigenous people. They must be able to doctor themselves and sometimes their study animals. They learn to be photographers and map makers. They must be able to stand loneliness. They must be able to stand being too wet, too dry, too cold or too hot.

Field biologists often remain at their study site in a foreign country to protect the animals they have come to know. They set up preserves and train local people to observe, protect and care for their wildlife using modern technology and management techniques.

Long-term studies are the key to successful fieldwork. Jane Goodall has been following the same troop of chimpanzees for thirty years. As a result, she knows family histories and has been able to learn much about chimp child care, birth and death. Had she not been able to stay for several decades at her study site, she might not have seen chimps use tools or eat meat and might not have witnessed the occasional wars the chimps wage with other groups.

Today, the boundaries between the zoo and the field are crossed again and again. The field biologists apply what has been learned in the zoo to understand animals in the wild. Information learned in the wild can be applied to improving life in the zoo.

What we have learned about the natural needs of wild animals is important to how we keep zoo animals. So much of what zoos are doing for environmental enrichment—giving attention to exhibit space, plantings in exhibits, social requirements and even providing the best vegetation—is learned by observing animals in the wild. How we apply what we learn about wild animals is of paramount

Dee Boersma has spent thousands of hours on the beaches of Patagonia tagging Humboldt penguins and counting their eggs.

Forest elephants in dense
growth near Fresco, Côte d'Ivoire, Africa.

Indian elephant Maxime, testing the collar that will be used
on forest elephants to track them in the dense growth of the
African forest. The collar sends signals indicating the location of the
elephant to a satellite, which sends information back to
Dr. Koontz's New York office.

An example of how research in the zoo is directly benefiting our understanding of a wild species involves two elephants: a forest elephant, a subspecies of the African elephant, in a national park in Cameroon and an Indian elephant at the Bronx Zoo/Wildlife Conservation Park.

It has been difficult to study the forest elephants because they are virtually impossible to see buried in the dense growth. In order to protect the elephants, it is important to know more about them and their range, how much space they need to get the food they require and the behavior of males, females and the young.

Now, James Powell of the Wildlife Conservation Society is in Cameroon tracking them through the use of a radio collar designed by Fred Koontz, curator of mammals, and tested on a captive elephant, Maxime, in the Bronx. Keepers tested the durability and adjusted the fit of the collar using Maxime. In this way they were better prepared to collar an elephant in the wild.

Drs. William Karesh and Hubert Planton, wildlife veterinarians, went to Africa and darted an elephant and collared it. The collar, designed to fall off after two years, sends a signal to a satellite that passes over Cameroon and can receive information twice a day. The signal goes via France to a computer screen in Dr. Koontz's New York office. Every evening, he checks the exact location of the wild elephant so he can pass on the information when needed to Dr. Powell in Cameroon. It takes a relay from Africa to New York to inform the staff in Africa that the elephant is nearby.

The signal also senses motion. Should the wild elephant stop moving, indicating serious injury or death, an anti-poaching patrol can be sent out quickly.

importance to making the SSPs successful.

Shirley Strum relocates an entire troop of baboons in order to protect them from the humans who had begun to take over their natural territory. She names them the "Pumphouse Gang."

Chuck Carr patrols the beaches of Central America with students and volunteers for poachers. They are protecting female sea turtles as they drag themselves painstakingly across the sand to lay their eggs. Chuck is also working with the governments of several Central American countries to provide safe passage for the panther, which needs free range of the land, no matter whose borders it crosses.

High in the mountains of Papua New Guinea, Mary Pearl talks with leaders of tribes—who not so long ago used only stone tools and knew nothing about the rest of the world—about the need to protect the fabulous wildlife and resources of their land from the logging companies and animal dealers that are robbing their natural wealth.

Dangling from a cliff in Seattle, Stan Temple hangs by a rope around the waist and reaches into the nest of a peregrine falcon to

Small group of females and young baboons.

Terese Hart
with okapi.

replace an egg, thereby making sure that one more chick will have a chance at survival.

Amy Samuels has spent a lifetime as a link between animals and humans. She has helped teach a nonverbal language to chimpanzees, working in a lab and in the field. Now a behavioral biologist at the Chicago Zoological Park, she travels to Hawaii and Cape Cod, following wild dolphins.

Drs. John and Terese Hart are American ecologists who have studied the okapi, or forest giraffe, and other wildlife in the Ituri

region of Zaire for nearly twenty years. It is not unusual to see them tracking an okapi, followed by a line of little girls in grass skirts, giggling and barefoot. Three of them are their daughters, raised among the natives of the Ituri forest.

Several zoos have field biologists on staff, and many other zoos help pay expenses for field studies. Many field biologists get support for their work from a combination of organizations such as universities and conservation organizations like the World Wildlife Fund. The AZA has a conservation and science division that monitors all the SSPs, field studies and the work of scientists around the world.

Although several zoos sponsor field research, one organization administered by a zoo is totally dedicated to field work: the global field division of the the Wildlife Conservation Society works in developing countries where biological diversity is greatest and pressure on nature most intense. Currently, it has the largest field operation of all international conservation organizations, with approximately 225 field programs in forty-six coun-

Wildlife
Conservation
Society map of
conservation
projects worldwide.
Currently, the
Wildlife
Conservation
Society has the
largest field
operation of all
international
conservation
organizations.

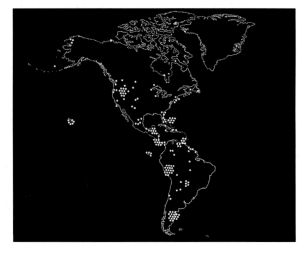

tries throughout Central and South America, Asia and Africa. As a result of the work of Wildlife Conservation Society field biologists, more than one hundred wildlife preserves have been established.

Dr. John G. Robinson became general director of the international conservation division of the Wildlife Conservation Society in 1990 from a background as a primatologist and has presided over a major expansion of the programs and staff.

GEORGE SCHALLER
Director for Science
1958–

Dr. George Schaller is perhaps responsible for protecting more wildlife than any other human being alive today.

His quest for understanding animals in their natural state began early in his life. Forty years ago, he completed the first study of mountain gorillas in the wild. With his wife Kay, he lived high in the mountains of Rwanda, recording observations until he got a full picture of the social life and personality of great apes. In large part because of his work, myths surrounding these gentle giants disappeared. Among the many keystone species Dr. Schaller has studied over his lifetime are the lions of the Serengeti in Africa, the snow leopards in Nepal and the giant pandas of China.

Until Dr. Schaller became involved, the wildlife of Tibet and Mongolia had been largely ignored. The Tibetan plateau is 830,000 square miles in size—as large as Alaska and Texas combined. The northwestern part, Chang Tang, remains mostly unsettled by humans because it is so high and bleak. Many large mammals live on the plateau, including the wild yak, Tibetan antelope, blue sheep, wolf, snow leopard and Tibetan brown bear. Where roads have advanced through the plateau, much of the wildlife has met the same fate as the bison on the American plains.

Dr. Schaller was invited by the Chinese government to study the geographical area and recommend what land could most productively be set aside as preserve. Because of his research, which involved climbing through bitterly cold terrain for months at a time, the Chang Tang Reserve was recently established, the world's second largest nature reserve, with 92,400 square miles (the largest is in Greenland and consists mostly of icecap).

In Dr. Schaller's words, "Conservation initiatives are usually made in response to crises—after wildlife has been decimated and habitat destroyed. The Chang Tang provides a unique opportunity to protect a large area and plan for its wise use before it has been damaged. Such an opportunity is indeed rare in today's world." Dr. George Schaller's next objective is to make certain that other adjoining areas are also protected, including the Memar Lake region just west of the Chang Tang Reserve, where Tibetan antelope females come to give birth.

George Schaller in China with captive giant panda.

Giant panda of China. George Schaller was responsible for establishing the world's second largest nature reserve—the Chang Tang Reserve, with 92,400 square miles.

ALAN RABINOWITZ
Director, Asia Program
1982–

Alan Rabinowitz lies quietly in the humid heat of dawn under his mosquito netting, savoring a few more moments of rest while he listens to the spirited sounds of tropical birds in their morning chorus.

A wildlife biologist with the Wildlife Conservation Society, one of many who work to establish wildlife preserves all over the world, he has another big day ahead. He is going to do what he had been planning for months before he left New York and for a year since arriving in Belize: capture a jaguar to put a radio collar on it.

The electronic signal from the collar can be followed from a great distance. Tracking is very important in finding answers. How far do the animals travel? How much land does each animal need? Do females behave differently from males? Which animals meet? Do they stay in the same territory all year long?

While the animal is tranquilized to apply the collar, other important information is gathered, including measurements and samples of blood and tissue. From toads to tapirs, animals can now be safely radio collared.

When Alan was able to collar his first jaguar, the resulting information was critical in establishing a preserve for the big cats in Belize. Because of his work with the jaguar, the governments of Belize and the United States have worked together to set aside territory where rare and beautiful animals are protected from hunters. Since doing research in Belize, Alan has studied the big cats of Asia.

AMY VEDDER
Director, Africa Program
1978–

Amy Vedder studied biology in college and then went on to join the Peace Corps in Africa. During this time in Zaire, Amy met her first gorilla. Few people even in Africa had ever seen a gorilla. For Amy and her husband, Bill Weber, it put their lives onto a new track. They wanted to understand more about gorillas.

As graduate students of conservation biology, Amy and Bill returned to Africa—this time to Rwanda—to study how the needs of the people and of the gorillas related. The gorilla population was thought to be declining because of habitat loss.

Alan Rabinowitz taking radio tracking information. The resulting information from tracking his first jaguar was critical in establishing a preserve for the big cats in Belize.

Amy Vedder outside her home and office in Rwanda, doing fieldwork study of the mountain gorilla.

Amy set out to do a census and an ecological assessment (a study of the gorilla food sources, the range of their territory and the space they were using in the territory). Her research corroborated Dian Fossey's work, showing that the gorilla population was in jeopardy not so much because of the destruction of their habitat but because they were being killed by poachers. They were innocent victims in the war the humans had fought for independence. Following the war, the people continued to poach the gorillas for food and souvenirs.

Amy and Bill persuaded the government that it could effectively protect the gorillas and promote ecotourism, which would encourage the people to recognize that their wildlife and land could be of great value, a natural resource. Today, tourists visiting the gorillas in the national parks in a controlled fashion bring money into the country and make the gorillas more valuable alive than dead. Many people in the region are employed by the park, and the number of gorillas is increasing.

MARY PEARL
**Former Director, Asia Program
Research Fellowship Program Manager
1986–1993**

Dr. Mary Pearl is, as a primatologist, an expert field biologist with a focus on the primates and conservation biology of Asia. She also trains students and coordinates research in America and Asia.

She studies what impact human activity has on the vegetation and primates. Working with botanists from the New York Botanical Garden, she is helping Asian people maximize food production without disturbing wildlife or cutting forests.

Mary is on the staff of the New York Consortium in Evolutionary Primatology, a graduate training program in the behavioral and evolutionary biology of primates. The program brings together faculty from several universities and uses the facilities of the American Museum of Natural History and the Wildlife Conservation Society to train students. The collaboration of these different

Baby mountain gorilla. The mountain gorilla has been the victim of poaching for many years.

Scarlet and red and green macaws at a salt lick in Peru. Approximately twenty thousand to fifty thousand macaws are captured every year for the pet trade. More than three-fourths of them die before they reach the pet store.

Charles Munn in
Manu National Park
with biologist
Benedicto Boca.

institutions allows students direct observation of the animals in the zoo setting in order to understand primates in their natural habitats. In 1993, Mary became director of Wildlife Preservation Trust International, an organization which trains field staffs around the world.

CHARLES MUNN
Research Zoologist
1983–

Dr. Munn has been working in the Manu region of southeastern Peru for ten years, gathering information on population, behavior and conservation needs of the flamboyant macaw. These beautiful birds had been captured for the pet trade until they were on the verge of extinction. It is estimated that of about fourteen million birds captured for the pet trade every year, twenty thousand to fifty thousand are macaws. More than three-fourths of them die before they reach the pet store.

Through Dr. Munn's research and his relationship with the local people, he has recently been able to establish a mutually beneficial arrangement.

The people of the native community of Tayakome have agreed not to capture macaws and Amazon parrots. In return, the village has received a short-wave transmitter—a transmitter especially valuable in medical emergencies.

Dr. Munn continues his work to protect those areas and to stem the trade in exotic birds.

FRED W. KOONTZ
Curator of Mammals
1984–

Dr. Koontz's father was a natural history buff who introduced Fred to the wonders of the natural world. As Fred got older, he was inspired by the work of Dr. Konrad Lorenz, the renowned Austrian ethologist.

As a first-year graduate student, he met Chris Wemmer and spent a summer at the National Zoo's Research and Conservation Center at Front Royal, Virginia. There he learned to track opossums, became familiar with biotelemetry and realized that the role of zoos was changing. Work in the wild, not the classroom, now inspired him.

Black howler
monkeys being
airlifted for
reintroduction into
the Cockscomb
Basin of Belize, once
their natural habitat.
The howler monkey
has been extinct in
this region for many
years due to
deforestation and
the native
population's
dependence on
them as a food
source. This project,
however, is proving
successful with four
new babies born the
first year and thirty
additional howlers
to be relocated
soon.

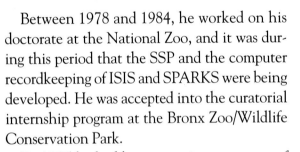

Between 1978 and 1984, he worked on his doctorate at the National Zoo, and it was during this period that the SSP and the computer recordkeeping of ISIS and SPARKS were being developed. He was accepted into the curatorial internship program at the Bronx Zoo/Wildlife Conservation Park.

By 1985 he had become assistant curator of mammals, and he saw ways in which his expertise with computers and animals could be combined. He started the biotelemetry studies unit through which the sensor in the crane egg and the tracking of the forest elephant described earlier came to be.

But now Fred is able to take his work yet another step: practice runs for reintroduction. Black howler monkeys once roamed throughout areas of Central America, the Yucatán, Belize and Guatemala. The forests of their natural habitat, an area called the Cockscomb Basin of Belize, are being cut down at an alarming rate. The howler monkey is also a food source for the native population. Fortunately, they still survive in another area of Belize, the Community Baboon Sanctuary in Bermucian Landing. In fact, many troops are there because

the village has been encouraged to develop ecotourism instead of hunting and logging and has created a wildlife sanctuary.

Now Fred and a team of field biologists have begun an experiment to reintroduce the wild howlers from the well-populated area to the area where they are extinct.

In the spring of 1992, they located several troops, set up cages in the forest and devised a plan to capture, airlift and release three entire troops of howlers. He planned for every detail, including finding an expert in tranquilizing howler monkeys with a dart gun. Early in the morning, the crew surrounded the trees where the monkeys slept. One by one, they were darted with tranquilizers, examined, fitted with transmitters and put into transport cages. By midmorning, all were on their way, fifty miles to their new home.

For a few days, they remained in large cages filled with local leaves and fruits, with people on guard against jaguars and other predators. Finally, they were released. And for the year since their release, they have made the general vicinity their range. Only one young female and one male have disappeared, perhaps prey

Top: Rhino management.

to a large cat. Within the first year, four babies were born. Thirty more howlers will soon be moved into the area.

This is an experiment, one step in learning the best ways to move animals into protected habitats. What is learned from this project will open the door to similar translocations of wild animals and reintroductions of SSP animals from zoos back into protected areas.

PATRICIA MOEHLMAN
Research Zoologist
1986–

Following an education at Wellesley College, the University of Texas and the University of Wisconsin, Dr. Moehlman, a behavioral ecologist, began studying the evolution of social systems, doing her fieldwork in Africa.

She has spent almost two decades in Tanzania, Africa, seven of them coordinating Wildlife Conservation Society programs. Her work includes environmental monitoring at reserves and national parks, training Tanzanian wildlife personnel in park management, working for protection of the black

rhinos and studying jackals.

She has collected data on the Ngorogoro conservation area for more than twenty years and has assessed the effects of fire, tourism and grazing by domestic cattle. In Somalia, she has studied the conservation of the Somalian wild ass, including the population distribution and genetics, and has helped to train local nomads on how to protect the region's wildlife.

Bottom: Black rhino: The populations of all five rhino species have declined precipitously. The cause in part is the expansion of human populations and habitat destruction, but since 1970 85 percent of the world's rhinos have been killed for their horns. The horns are ground up and used in traditional medicines and as artifacts, bringing as much as $700 per pound.

In Africa the number of black rhino has plunged from 65,000 to 2,500 in less than 20 years, victims of poachers. Once found throughout the African savanna, the black rhino survives only in isolated pockets of Zimbabwe, South Africa, Kenya, Namibia and Tanzania.

Chapter Nine
GOING HOME

Thanks to the work of field biologists, veterinarians, curators, keepers, the local governments and geneticists, some animals have been pulled away from the edge of extinction and can go back into their natural habitats: the California condor, black-footed ferret, Arabian oryx, Bali mynah, golden lion tamarin, Puerto Rican crested toad, red wolf and thick-billed parrot. For these animals, the Species Survival Plan is working. The animals are breeding

well in zoos and babies are being born. Protected or safe areas have been found for them in their native habitats.

Most zoo animals have been fed regularly and receive regular medical attention. They are protected from the harsh elements and they have not been hunted by predators. Going back into nature can be very difficult for animals who have been born and raised in the protected circumstances of the zoo. Most animals being reintroduced must be trained to return to life outside. Even if they still have their natural instincts going for them, this training is crucial to being able to cope in the wild.

How this is done depends on the species. Generally, there is some sort of halfway place where the animals can acclimate gradually to

the new environment. Eventually, they are on their own, although the field biologists will track them and observe them over time.

The following are examples of some successful reintroductions.

REINTRODUCTIONS AROUND THE WORLD
Arabian Oryx
SSP Coordinators: Jim Dolan,
San Diego Zoo
Karen Sausman, The Living Desert

Looking out over the desert at the silhouette of an Arabian oryx traced against the sky, it is easy to imagine unicorns. From the side, the two long, straight horns could easily be seen as one magical horn on the elegant head. For their horns and for their skins, Arabian oryx have been hunted for generations. In the age of four-wheel drive and long-range rifles, they did not stand a chance. By 1972, not one oryx survived in the wild.

Fortunately, when the plight of the oryx became evident, several countries had the foresight to gather a "world herd" of Arabian oryx. One animal came from the London Zoo, three from the Oman border, four from the king of Saudi Arabia and one from the emir of Kuwait. The group was sent to the Phoenix Zoo in the hope that the dry climate of Arizona would be enough like Arabia that the animals would do well and breed.

A second breeding group was sent from the zoo in Riyadh, Saudi Arabia, to the Los Angeles Zoo. By 1971, there were thirty-one animals in the world herd. Some went to the San Diego Wild Animal Park. Since then, the number of zoos in North America that keep Arabian oryx and participate in the SSP has grown to twenty. By 1977, there were several hundred animals in the world herd, and a reintroduction was attempted. They were acclimated in an enclosure in Oman and finally released. Today, they are also in six other middle eastern countries.

ARUBA ISLAND RATTLESNAKE
also known as ARUBA CASCABEL
SSP Coordinator: S. Andrew Odum, Toledo Zoo

Cactus scrub, sandy soil and rocks baking in a hot Caribbean sun—the Aruba Island rattlesnake calls it home. On Aruba, an island about fifteen miles off the coast of Venezuela, hotels, roads, clubs and all the other effects of increased civilization have destroyed the nat-

Arabian oryx.

ural habitat. Trees have been cut for firewood and charcoal. Introduction of domestic goats has destroyed any remaining vegetation. Except for the human sun worshippers, the island has been destroyed for most of its wildlife. The rattlesnake is no exception.

No one knows how many of these snakes still exist, but they are listed as threatened in the IUCN Red Data Book and by the U.S. Fish and Wildlife Service. Although it is illegal to export the snakes from the island, they have no other protection, and they are killed for their rattles.

The area where they do survive is ten square miles of relatively undisturbed habitat, inhospitable to humans but home to the snakes, lizards, frogs, birds and a few mammals.

American scientists and educators have gone to Aruba to study the wildlife. They have established programs to teach the value of the snake in controlling the rodent population and the other ways it is part of the natural web. The snakes are also contributing to the study of antivenoms.

Recently, ten snakes were caught in a resi-dential area. Instead of being destroyed as they would have been in years past, they were presented to the SSP to improve genetic diversity in the program. The goal is to have 250 snakes in the program. Currently there are one hundred.

The Aruba Island Rattlesnake SSP is an example of how an animal not greatly loved has, nonetheless, been given protection for its value as a part of a natural habitat. The people of Aruba now take pride in the snake; the Aruba Island rattlesnake is pictured on postage stamps and new currency.

BALI MYNAH
also known as ROTHSCHILD'S STARLING or JALAK BALI
SSP Coordinator: Robert Siebels, Riverbanks Zoological Garden

Like a snow fairy, the Bali mynah is a shimmering white bird the size of a starling. Startling blue rings circle piercing dark eyes, and black tips accent the elegant wings. A long, lacy tuft rises on the head in courtship displays. The Bali mynah has become a symbol of conservation in Indonesia. This magnif-

Aruba Island rattlesnake. Since the SSP program began protecting the rattlesnake the people of Aruba have learned to appreciate the value of this indigenous reptile.

Bali mynah—native habitat Indonesia. If not for the intervention of a collective zoo effort from around the world the Bali mynah would be extinct. By 1990 the remaining population numbered just twenty. A prized bird of the pet trade, the Bali mynah is often a victim of poachers. The Bali mynah is now a member of the AZA's SSP program. There are currently fifty-five to sixty birds living in the wild due to the efforts of the SSP.

icent bird would no longer exist if zoos around the world had not stepped in to block the certain path to extinction. In 1990, the remaining wild population numbered just twenty.

Because the Bali mynah is prized as a cage bird, the pet trade around the globe is largely responsible for bringing the wild population to such tiny numbers. The birds are prime targets for poachers.

These elegant birds are indigenous to a very small portion of Indonesia and nest in tree hollows. Soaring human populations and the clearing of land for coconut plantations and firewood have put Bali mynah housing at a premium.

Alerted to the crisis by the Indonesian government in 1982, the AZA created a studbook for the captive Bali mynah. Only five years later, thirty-nine captive-bred birds from U.S. zoos were sent to Surabaya Zoo in Java. One year after that, the first of this group's offspring were released into Bali Barat National Park.

As in other reintroductions, the birds are not just taken from the zoo and let go in the protected park. The birds are hatched in North American zoos after careful consideration of the best genetic combinations. The adults are then sent to Surabaya Zoo in Indonesia. The birds born to these adults are sent to a semi-wild preserve in Bali Barat National Park. The birds who go to Bali Barat are fledged: they have left the nest and are independent of their parents but are still young and adaptable.

They live in a sheltered area but have no contact with humans. The berries and fruits which they will find to eat once they are released are supplied for a time. Bali mynahs live in communities. The time spent at the preserve allows them to form social ties. Once their human guardians feel that the birds can find food for themselves and they appear to be healthy and at ease in a natural habitat, they are released in groups of ten to twelve into the park. The birds are banded and implanted with transponders so that they can be followed. Transponders are like little computer chips which can be scanned like items at the grocery store. Already it has proven worthwhile. Through an undercover operation a bird was discovered in a black market pet store. Although the store owner denied the bird was wild, a quick scan proved him wrong. The bird was taken and returned to the freedom of Bali Barat.

The thirteen mynahs released so far seem to be doing very well, interacting with the wild flock, even breeding. In 1993, there were fifty-five to sixty birds in the wild. Nearly one thousand birds are well and genetically intact in zoos around the world.

Zoos in North America and Indonesia, along with the International Council for Bird Preservation, the Nature Conservation Service of Indonesia and the Jersey Wildlife Trust, have all participated to assure the survival of the Bali mynah.

GOLDEN LION TAMARIN
SSP Coordinator: Jon Ballou,
National Zoological Park
Reintroduction: Benjamin Beck, National
Zoological Park
Research: Devra Kleiman, National Zoo
James Dietz, University of Maryland

Cars whiz by Rock Creek Park in Washington, D.C. Drivers noticing a brilliant flash of orange springing through the trees might think it is a red squirrel or a brilliant bird. Surely they would not suspect that this tiny creature with the wise face, the flowing mustache and the perfect little hands is a primate.

But it is. This flash of orange is a golden lion tamarin. And in a flash its kind might disappear forever from the world. But for now, it hops about in the trees surrounding the National Zoo in preparation for its return home to Brazil, South America. The golden lion tamarin was one of the first to benefit from global cooperation and the reintroduction of endangered species to their natural homes.

Once, golden lion tamarins ranged over millions of acres of forest in Brazil. The intense clear-cutting of the trees for farms and

Golden lion tamarin
twins riding on the back
of their father.
The golden lion tamarin
was one of the first to
benefit from global
cooperation and the
reintroduction program.

ranches and the spread of the big city Rio de Janeiro destroyed most of their natural home. And these beautiful, active animals were captured for sale as pets or zoo animals. The future looked grim.

In 1970, there were only two hundred golden lion tamarins living in the little bit of forest which remained. The population in zoos numbered only seventy, and they were dying. They became sick with respiratory illnesses, intestinal troubles and even measles. Very few babies were being born, and those that were died of rickets, a vitamin D deficiency. Away from their natural habitat and fed a poor diet, their vivid coats became a dull yellow.

No one understood these energetic animals, and certainly they would have disappeared from the earth had not one man, Adelmar F. Coimbra-Filho, on the staff of the zoo in Rio de Janeiro, bothered to speak up for the golden lion tamarins. At a meeting on the problems of conservation in Brazil, he asked that the little primates be added to the Red Data Book to prevent trapping or importing of the endangered animals.

Until then, zoos were still competing for animals. But faced with the immediate loss of the tamarins, zoos banded together to find ways to save them. Rather than guarding secrets about breeding and feeding, zoos began cooperating. All of the captive tamarins in North America were distributed to twenty-five zoos but were owned by only five.

Research into the animal's behavior and physical needs paid off. It had been assumed that the tropical primates required large quantities of fruit. It turned out that they needed a balance in their diet, mostly more protein from insects and lizards. As soon as the young animals got more sunshine and food rich in vitamin D, rickets was no longer a problem.

Zoo behaviorists learned that tamarin families stay together until the adolescents move off to start their own families. Young females often leave home first. This is unlike most other primate species.

Soon, infants were living, and the fathers were carrying them around as is their nature.

By 1981, through the efforts of scientists and conservation groups in North America and Brazil, Poco das Antas, a modest reserve, had been set aside for the tamarins, large enough to protect the animals still living there and, it was hoped, the many animals being born in zoos as well. The National Zoo began to introduce the golden lion tamarins gradually to the natural outdoors. That is why they can be seen flitting through trees around the zoo.

In 1983, the first group of fifteen tamarins was sent to Brazil. At first, they stayed in a large enclosure to get used to the sounds, smells and feeling of their new home. When they were finally on their own, they wore tiny radio transmitters so that researchers could track them.

As of 1993, 141 golden lion tamarins had been reintroduced and fifty-two were still alive. In all, almost three hundred golden lion tamarins are living in the Poco das Antas Reserve in Brazil.

REINTRODUCTIONS IN NORTH AMERICA

For most animals in the SSPs, there are animals in captivity, in zoos or private ownership and at least a small number in the wild.

But in some cases, the situation is discovered only when the animals are at the brink of extinction. This was the case for both the black-footed ferret and the California condor. The few remaining animals living in the wild were captured and brought into captivity to breed. There is a great deal of controversy about taking the last animals from the wild to put into a zoo—even to save the species. It is an extreme measure for an extreme situation.

BLACK-FOOTED FERRET
SSP Coordinator: E. Tom Thorne,
Wyoming Game and Fish Department

Once there were thousands of black-footed ferrets in at least twelve of the western United States and two Canadian provinces. They caused no trouble; they hunted prairie dogs and lived in their burrows. Cattle ranchers

Black-footed ferret—there were once thousands of these small mammals living in at least twelve of the western United States and two Canadian provinces. Poisoned to near extinction because they ate prairie dogs that were poisoned by cattle ranchers, under the SSP program there is hope that in several years there will be a new population of 1,500 black-footed ferrets in nine locations throughout the west and that they can once again live and breed on their own as part of the prairie ecosystem.

and farmers did not like prairie dogs because their cattle stepped in the burrows, risking broken legs. They poisoned as many as they could, nearly wiping them out. With so few prairie dogs, black-footed ferrets starved to death.

They were thought to be already extinct when a few small colonies of these long, slinky, masked mammals were located by persistent scientists. But then disaster struck anew. An epidemic of distemper hit them—perhaps transmitted by wild dogs.

The remaining animals began to die at an alarming rate. Scientists were certain that there were none left. A biologist, Conrad Hillman, searched abandoned prairie dog burrows at night by flashlight for four years, not finding a single black-footed ferret. The verdict seemed clear: they were extinct.

Then, in 1986, eighteen were discovered in Wyoming. It was big news. Some experts wanted to trap them and bring them into captivity so they would survive and breed. Others argued that it was wrong to capture them, no matter why—they belonged in the wild. Finally, it was decided to bring them into captivity for breeding, prior to reintroduction to the wild. The Henry Doorly Zoo, the National Zoo's Conservation and Research Center in Front Royal, Virginia, and the Sybille Wildlife Research and Conservation Unit in Wheatland, Wyoming, have been homes for the animals. The Phoenix and Metro Toronto Zoos joined the SSP for black-footed ferrets in 1993.

The breeding program is going well, and from the sixteen founders there are now 325 black-footed ferrets in captivity, and forty-nine—vaccinated against distemper—have been reintroduced into a 140,000-acre site owned by the federal government and private owners in south central Wyoming. And no one will try to control the prairie dogs without letting the ferret scientists know.

To prepare the ferrets for the dangers of life on the outside, the research scientists have invented a way to teach them about one of their natural enemies—the badger. Technicians devised "RoboBadger," a mechanical badger that frightened the heck out of those ferrets that were born in a nest box.

The animals (as prepared as could be) were released at the age of eighteen months. At this age the animals are mature enough to take care of themselves but are still capable of adapting to the wild. They were taken to the location in the nest boxes they were raised in. After ten days, the doors were left open and they were free to come and go. Food was left for them for ten more days. Some returned to the nest box a few nights, others just kept on going.

It is expected that many will be lost to badgers and coyotes, so for the next three or four years fifty more youngsters will be released. The hope is that in several years there will be a population of 1,500 black-footed ferrets in nine locations throughout the west and that they can once again live and breed on their own as part of the prairie ecosystem.

CALIFORNIA CONDOR
SSP Coordinator: Michael Wallace,
Los Angeles Zoo

The bald, bright red head and neck are shadowed by the powerful stretch of black wings spread wide to catch the wind currents high above California. Here, above the rugged mountains of the Sespe Condor Sanctuary seventy-five miles from Los Angeles, the first California condors to fly free since 1987 are to be released. After ten years of breeding them in captivity, members of the California condor recovery team are ready to take the risk.

For a million years, these magnificent birds soared above North America. They are vultures and therefore eat carrion, carcasses of animals.

Human overpopulation forced California condors out of their natural range. They flew into power lines and were the targets of shootings. Unintentionally, humans killed these birds with poisons: pesticides weakened the shells of their eggs so they cracked too early; they ate the flesh of poisoned coyotes; they died from lead poisoning caused by eating animals killed with lead pellets of shotguns.

As with the black-footed ferret, the last

known California condors were rounded up and brought into captivity.

Because the San Diego and Los Angeles Zoos had twenty-seven condors already in captivity, a breeding program could begin.

Two eight-month-old California condors are being prepared for the wild by living in outcroppings covered by a huge net. They are being fed by the researchers and will continue to be fed for some time so that they do not risk poisoning again. As chicks, they had to be fed by a human hand gloved in a condor puppet. Since birds imprint on what they first see upon hatching and as young chicks, it was important not to have them bond to humans.

Today there are fifty-two California condors in captivity, none in the wild. The last-known wild California condor, AC-9, has fathered five of the chicks born in captivity. One of those is among the first to be released. The genetic diversity of the chicks is very good, and the recovery team is optimistic that eventually there will be two separate wild populations of one hundred birds each.

Condor chick at the Los Angeles Zoo being fed by a human hand gloved in a condor puppet. Since birds imprint on what they first see upon hatching and as young chicks, it was important not to have them bond to humans.

The California condor has been brought to near extinction due to a number of factors: human overpopulation, pesticides which weakened the shells of their eggs and poisoning by eating the remains of animals killed by lead pellets of shotguns.

California condor.

Chapter Ten

WHO IS WATCHING OUT
FOR THE ANIMALS?

ANIMAL WELFARE ORGANIZATIONS

North Americans have a much greater awareness and sensitivity for

animal welfare today than they did even as recently as twenty years

ago. Many organizations have been created to look out for the animals, each with

a slightly different focus.

These include the American Society for the Prevention of Cruelty to Animals

(ASPCA), the American Humane Association (AHA), the Humane Society of the United States (HSUS), the Fund for Animals and the Animal Welfare Institute.

They are constituted to educate people about the issues, to create laws and other protective measures for animals and to give direct care. Each has a staff that includes a director and many people working as writers, lawyers, publicists and veterinarians. A direct-care group would also have kennel cleaners or caretakers for injured wildlife.

Most animal welfare organizations have as their primary mission the welfare of domestic animals: dogs, cats and farm animals. Some are concerned also with exotic wildlife. They may be very large organizations active in creating laws to protect animals, in organizing humane-education programs and in employing animal officers who rescue animals from abusive situations. Or they may be as small as a local animal shelter.

The American Humane Association

For 115 years, the American Humane Association (AHA) has been finding and fighting the causes of suffering and abuse of animals, as well as of children. In 1877, the twenty-seven humane agencies that existed united to become the first national organization to protect animals from neglect, abuse and exploitation. In 1885, they expanded their efforts to work for the welfare of children.

Since then, they have organized the American Red Star Animal Relief Program. Like the

The Humane Society of the United States put together the following checklist to help you decide if the zoo you are visiting is a professional conservation center or a roadside zoo/menagerie:

- Did you learn anything about the wildlife or its habitat from your visit?
- Were the exhibits and grounds clean? Did the animals appear clean and healthy?
- Were fresh water and shade available? Protection from the weather? Did the animals look well fed?
- Were the exhibits interesting and did the animals have opportunities for activity—i.e., could climbing animals climb and swimming animals swim?
- Did the animals have places to hide from view in their exhibits or were they constantly exposed to public scrutiny?
- Were there keepers or other zoo staff members or volunteer workers close by to answer your questions and insure that visitors did nothing to harm the animals? Did they seem knowledgeable and concerned about the animals?
- Are there twenty-four-hour security guards or a high fence enclosing the entire zoo to protect the animals from vandals when the zoo is closed?
- What percentage of the zoo is made up of old-fashioned barred, sterile cages?
- Are there plans to modernize outmoded exhibits to make them more naturalistic and provide the animals with more opportunities for activity? In what period of time will these changes be made?
- Does the zoo provide special educational programs for visitors who wish to learn more about animals?
- Is there a zoological society you can join to help see that improvements are made and educational programs are developed?

Animal rights
organizations fight
against such
inhumane displays
of animals.

Red Cross for humans, the Red Star provides care for animals in times of natural disaster, with human volunteers, medical treatment, shelter and food.

They also were the first group to look out for the welfare of animal "actors." Before groups like AHA brought attention to the film industry, horses could be forced off cliffs, made to fall with trip wires and used in many ways to create realism in the film without any concern for their safety.

AHA continues the battle against pet overpopulation and acts as an advocate for the humane treatment of farm animals, marine and other wildlife, pets, animals in the entertainment industry and laboratory

A roadside menagerie—such displays of animals still exist.

ROADSIDE ZOOS

Unfortunately, menageries still exist, some in the form of roadside zoos, announced perhaps by something like a big sign saying WILLY'S WILD ANIMAL WONDER LAND, with a huge cutout of a ferocious gorilla with flashing teeth.

A visitor will probably not find a gorilla at Willy's but will find Willy selling gasoline and souvenirs and maybe see a young chimpanzee with a chain around its neck attached to a pole in the ground. It has no protection from the sun, there is no water and there are feces all over the ground.

Although animal welfare groups and AZA-accredited zoos disagree on many things, they do agree that these establishments have no place in our world. Modern menageries or roadside zoos are a disgrace. In most cases they are also illegal.

There are more than 1,500 places registered with the Department of Agriculture as animal facilities (only 162 are AZA zoos). However, this number changes regularly as zoos are added and removed from the AZA accreditation list. Probably thousands more exist unregistered. There are more places with animals than can possibly be properly supervised.

animals, as well as for child welfare.

Recently, they have been studying the link between abuses of animals and children. Working with experts from animal protection, child welfare, law, medicine, psychology and related fields, they have shown that animal abuse is an indicator of other abuse going on in the human family.

The American Society for the Prevention of Cruelty to Animals

"Stop it, stop it I say. Stop whipping that horse!" A well-dressed gentleman raced over to grab the arm of a wagon driver who was savagely beating his fallen horse. Henry Bergh did the unthinkable for the 1860s in America: he spoke up for an animal.

By stopping the abuse of a horse, Mr. Bergh started Americans on a path that continues today—protecting the rights and the welfare of animals. Mr. Bergh's outrage took shape to become the American Society for the Prevention of Cruelty to Animals. Founded by Mr. Bergh in 1866, the ASPCA worked to give animals protection from people who felt they could do whatever they liked to the animals they owned.

As it had done with zoological gardens, the United States followed the British example. Mr. Bergh based the creation of the ASPCA on the Royal Society for the Protection of Animals in Great Britain. He worked tirelessly to create and enforce laws to protect animals. It was a new concept to many people that individual animals had both physical and emotional feelings analogous to those of humans and that they should have rights to decent treatment.

The Humane Society of the United States

The Humane Society of the United States (HSUS) was founded in 1954 for the prevention of cruelty to animals. The founders realized the need to encourage and assist communities across America in establishing humane societies to work together toward eliminating cruelties to animals in slaughterhouses and medical research laboratories

and the uncontrolled breeding of pets.

By producing written material and films about the issues, HSUS educates the public and lawmakers. For example, their campaign "Beautiful Choice" brought to the public's attention the suffering of animals used to test cosmetic products, thereby forcing the beauty industry to change its practice of using live animals in painful research.

HSUS draws attention to the need for spaying and neutering programs for cats and dogs in order to curb pet overpopulation, the need to ban inhumane trapping and the need to search out other cases of animal suffering and abuse in zoos, the military, industry and schools. They are also assisting international conservation efforts. HSUS recently funded research to find more birth control means for exotic and domestic animals.

ZOOCHECK

ZOOCHECK, with offices in both England and Canada, is an organization that exists specifically to monitor zoos. For the past six years, it has been monitoring zoos to make sure that they meet standards set down by the CAZPA (Canadian Association of Zoological Parks and Aquariums) and, if they do not meet the standards, help them correct the situation or force the zoo to close down. ZOOCHECK also hosts lectures by wildlife authorities.

The American Association of Zoological Parks and Aquariums

Zoos themselves, of course, are interested in assuring that the animals in their facilities are well cared for. One reason for the creation of the American Association of Zoological Parks and Aquariums (AAZPA) was to encourage zoos to work together to develop standards and the best possible collaborative ideas to benefit their animals.

In the late sixties and early seventies, American zoos were considered part of the National Recreation and Parks Association (NRPA). Prior to that, zoo directors had been included in the American Institute of Park

Executives. Since first being included in the NRPA, zoos had grown in number and complexity. The business of caring for animals had become quite sophisticated. Zoo professionals were experts in managing captive wildlife and in operating a zoological facility. By the early 1970s, there were enough zoos and enough zoo professionals with concerns that went beyond those of the NRPA. Zoo professionals felt that they no longer belonged as a part of parks and voted to become independent. On January 19, 1972, it became official: zoo professionals had their own organization, the American Association of Zoological Parks and Aquariums, with 135 individual members.

By 1993, there were 162 accredited member zoos, plus individual members—people who work in zoos, companies that make zoo products like feed or fences, as well as individuals outside of the zoo community who are interested in conservation issues. This brings the total individual membership to 6,500. In October 1993, the organization shortened its name to American Zoo and Aquarium Association (AZA), but its responsibilities keep growing. Not every zoo can belong to the AZA. Zoos have to apply for accreditation. A team of professional zoo people investigate the applicant zoo. The team includes directors, veterinarians, business managers and curators, the people who manage the animals.

This team visits the zoo several times to scrutinize all areas, including administration, hospital records, bookkeeping, education, visitor services and the qualifications of the staff.

There is an ethics committee to evaluate the organization: what they do with surplus animals, training of animals, management problems. AZA has a conservation and science office devoted entirely to overseeing conservation programs.

Once accredited, a zoo is reviewed every five years to make sure that it meets AZA standards. (They can be dropped, and it happens.) Visitors may notice if a zoo is accredited. Generally there is a sign at the entrance. There is also a list at the back of this book.

There is a similar organization in Canada:

the Canadian Association of Zoological Parks and Aquariums. The American and Canadian associations cooperate on many levels. Several zoos hold memberships in both.

CONSERVATION ORGANIZATIONS

Conservation organizations such as World Wildlife Fund (WWF), the Sierra Club and Greenpeace work to protect plants and animals and their habitats from extinction. They may be governmental or private. These groups got started in Europe and North America in the nineteenth century as a response to the outrageous slaughter of birds to extinction for ladies' hats and of fur animals like seals for coats.

Some organizations are very specialized, like the Wolf Fund, which is concerned with the reintroduction of the wolf into Yellowstone National Park, or Trout Unlimited, dedicated to the protection of clean water and the enhancement of trout, salmon and steelhead fishery resources. Other conservation organizations are generalized and concerned with conservation issues ranging from habitat protection to acid rain.

Like animal welfare organizations, they work to protect animals by lobbying for laws and focusing on particular projects. As zoos have evolved to protect animals in the wild, they often overlap with the work of conservation organizations.

Over the decades there has been a great deal of debate between zoos and animal advocates. Basically, animal welfare groups focus on the protection of the individual animal, while zoos focus on the protection of the species. Often, they aren't well informed about what the other is doing.

Because of the crisis we face, there is little time for finger-pointing or criticism. Resources and time are very limited, and cooperation is the key. Fortunately in many instances, zoos and animal welfare agencies are working together to stop the capture of wild animals for pets, as typified by HSUS and AZA working together to inform the public about the travesty of the endangered-bird pet trade. Other examples are the cooperation between the AHA and the AZA to create guidelines for zoo animals being used in schools for educational purposes, zoos lobbying for stricter enforcement of the international wildlife agreement CITIES and the Audubon Society using zoos to get the conservation message to the public.

The Species Survival Commission (SSC) is part of IUCN. The goal of this international group is to conserve biological diversity by developing and implementing programs to save, restore and manage species and their habitat. Dr. George Rabb, director of the Brookfield Zoo in Chicago, is also director of SSC.

LAWS

Animal welfare and conservation organizations work to have laws enacted to make certain that animals, domestic or wild, are protected from abusive situations.

National Laws

The most comprehensive national law to protect animals in the United States is the Animal Welfare Act, enacted by Congress in 1966 as a result of the work of animal welfare organizations. Until then, there was little that could be done to stop mistreatment. Animals could not protest their treatment; instead, they got sick and often died.

The Animal Welfare Act directs the Department of Agriculture to maintain regulations which make certain that exotic and domestic animals are kept in safe, healthy, clean conditions, have adequate care when they travel and receive appropriate veterinary services.

The original act was written primarily to protect farm and laboratory animals. It was not until four years later, in 1970, that the regulations were expanded to include the caging and care of wild animals, to protect animals in roadside zoos as well as those in accredited zoos.

Not all animals are covered by the regulations, since the needs of many exotic animals are not known by the Department of Agriculture. Some of the regulations are vague, with loopholes that could allow continued inhumane treatment. The ethics of animal care are not considered.

In other words, it is as though you lived at home under rules that dictated what and how much you needed to eat every day, how big your room had to be, how many times a week you had to be walked around the yard and what medical care you had to receive. But no rules were established about hugs, or friends, or things to do or explore or learn. You would not be a really complete and comfortable human being.

Only recently were the regulations rewritten to consider the psychological well-being of primates—monkeys and great apes. This major advance recognized that there is more to animal health than just basic physical care; the mind of an animal also needs attention. It is a start.

These laws regulate any place that has animals for public display, but of course they are not always enforced. Some animals still exist in awful conditions, like in a menagerie, and suffer. There are several reasons why these conditions are allowed to exist:

THREATENED: Determined by a review of many factors: change in numbers of the species, the degree and type of threat, the limits of habitat, the level of conservation commitment.

ENDANGERED: Assured of extinction if any of the factors defining threatened get worse.

—From the IUCN Red List of Threatened Species

- There is not enough money to hire people to work for more laws.
- There are not enough inspectors to enforce the laws.
- The regulations are often not strict enough.
- The penalties are not severe enough.
- There is concern about what can be done with the animals if the facility is shut down and where they would go for care.
- The public does not speak out about poor conditions because either they do not know what is illegal or they do not know where to report it.

International Laws

The single most important international wildlife agreement is the Convention on International Trade in Endangered Species of Wild Fauna (animals) and Flora (plants) (CITIES). It was created by the International Union for the Conservation of Nature and Natural Resources (IUCN). By 1990, 105 nations had signed the agreement, the purpose of which is to allow controlled trade in animals and animal products (skins, feathers, etc.) which are not endangered while prohibiting trade in endangered animals.

In the CITIES agreement, all animals and plants known to science are divided into groups: Appendix I, II, and III. The more than six hundred species of animal and plant listed in Appendix I are endangered, and trade is strictly prohibited except in very special cases for research.

Appendix II can be thought of as a "waiting list." Plants and animals whose numbers are threatened are listed. Trade is permitted only if it is legal in the country they come from, the country of origin.

Appendix III lists plants and animals that are protected by their country of origin. Permits must be issued to countries wanting to import such fauna and flora. This is to curtail visitors—scientists, tourists, researchers— from casually taking any of these living things from their native habitat.

Of course, this agreement has major implications for zoos. Wild animals listed in Appendix I of CITIES cannot be trapped, traded or exported from their country of origin. Those in Appendix II or III must go through a complex permitting procedure to be exported, and even then, permission may be denied.

Unfortunately, there is a loophole in CITIES. Any signing country may take an exception to a species on the list. This loophole has allowed some countries to trade openly in endangered species.

The Unites States enforces CITIES through the Endangered Species Act (ESA), which prohibits trading, killing, capturing, trapping or even chasing a CITIES species without the proper permits. It is the job of the U.S. Fish and Wildlife Service to enforce this law, which must be reauthorized every four years, a requirement that gives opponents repeated opportunities to soften the law and to exempt species. It forces conservation-minded people to fight again and again to sustain the law.

Other laws in the United States regulate wildlife trade. Among them are the Marine Mammal Protection Act, which outlaws trade in sea mammals, the Migratory Bird Treaty Act, which limits trade in wild birds native to the U.S., and the Lacey Act, which makes it illegal for an American to buy any animal that has been illegally taken out of its country of origin. Fines have been increased, running as high as $20,000, with jail sentences up to five years for each offense.

In the U.S., the Lacey Act controls the unregulated killing of wildlife, such as the shooting of plumed birds for their feathers. It prohibits the interstate transport of wildlife killed in violation of a state law. It also allows a state to prohibit import of a lawfully killed animal.

But laws cannot be enforced if the public accepts poor standards of care. Important ethical aspects of animal care, from pet overpopulation to poor caging, cannot be legislated effectively. They will come to pass only if the public is informed and active in enforcing change.

Chapter Eleven
SUMMARY AND CONCLUSION

For thousands of years, zoos have been a part of world culture, reflecting human attitudes toward wildlife. Over the centuries, zoos have changed in name and focus from menagerie and postage stamp collection to zoological garden and conservation center. Nobility once displayed their captive animals in menageries to impress their guests. As humankind began to travel and came face-to-face with the wealth of species in the world, zoos organized their animal collections taxonomically or by species. These postage stamp exhibits emphasized the tremendous variety of animals found throughout the world. Today, the most creative zoos display entire ecosystems, reflecting human understanding of and concern for the earth as an interconnected system.

Zoos have made huge leaps in evolution since the day the elephant arrived at the Tower of London and was imprisoned for its lifetime. Keeping solitary animals in tile cages surrounded by bars is no longer tolerated. Instead, attempts are made to build natural environments and provide animals with social groups and enrichment so that they can live a near-normal life. Today, animals dwindling to extinction are taken from the wild, their breeding carefully managed with the hope of reintroducing them into the wild when the population numbers are stable and their habitat is safe.

Historically, animal collections and zoos have primarily been places for human entertainment, with little regard for animal welfare. It is only in the past two decades, as concern for and understanding of animal populations and their habitats has grown, that accredited zoos have become centers of environmental education and conservation research.

It would be wonderful if at this time in history there were no need for exotic animals to be kept in captivity, or if all facilities for captive animals were maintained with care and respect. But zoos are a reality. Until the day when there is no longer the threat of habitat destruction, poaching or death from disease introduced by humans, zoos in some form will have to fulfill their mission of conservation, education and research.

Rapid growth of the world's human population puts increasing pressure on the remaining natural regions of the earth. Wars, agriculture, forestry, hunting, housing, pollution and disease are taking a continual toll on wildlife populations and their habitats. There are fewer and fewer places on earth that remain undisturbed by humans. As the natural habitats which support wildlife populations become smaller, and the remaining animal populations are fragmented, there is an urgent need to manage what remains. Zoos have become keepers of the animals in a very different way than they once were.

In the past, our natural environment was largely taken for granted. The world's resources, including the animal kingdom, seemed limitless. Humans saw themselves as masters of the earth and separate from all other species. Today we have come to understand how closely related man is to the other animals of the earth and how dependent we all are on a healthy environment. Zoos have become leaders of environmental awareness.

Zoos practice conservation in the most basic and broadest senses of the word. On a most fundamental level, they are involved in preserving entire species, protecting individual animals and collecting the genetic material required to keep producing these animals. The modern technology of frozen zoos and embryo transplants has allowed the birth of babies from parents who are oceans apart.

The techniques and skills being developed at modern zoos are increasingly applied to help manage large wildlife preserves. Part of the management plan must include the healing of the animals' natural habitats. Repairing entire ecosystems, called "restoration ecology," is an area of growing interest and concern in zoos.

The dramatic change in human perspective on animals is resulting in the blurring of distinctions between zoos and the wild. Animal professionals, including vets, exhibit designers and field biologists, move easily back and forth, decreasing the differences between the kinds of care animals receive in each environment. The zoos have become laboratories for the development of new management techniques, and training grounds for an entire range of professionals.

Perhaps the next evolutionary step for zoos, which is already being considered by wildlife and environmental professionals, is the management of the earth's "biodiversity"—including the entire spectrum of living things together with the dynamic systems—as biological diversity parks. These "bioparks" would be places where habitats and species would be protected in restored ecosystems, where embryos of endangered species frozen today could be born. Where your great-grandchildren would still be able to marvel at the migration of the wildebeests stampeding over the African plain and smile at the bright faces of tamarin twins riding on their father's back through the rain forest of Brazil.

Who knows?

Afterword by
Terry Maple, Ph.D.

🐎

Linda Koebner's *Zoo Book* is the story of a new breed of conservationists. These "new conservationists" are the men and women employed by accredited zoos and aquariums who work on behalf of the world's wildlife. They are competent, diligent and energized. They will expend all of their skills and resources to combat the terrible forces of extinction. Admittedly, some major battles have been lost, but the war itself is far too important to be surrendered.

Today's accredited zoos and aquariums reach hundreds of millions of people annually, touching their lives with formal and informal messages of hope. Zoos can be inspiring locales where batteries are charged and spirits uplifted. Zoos must continue to report successful conservation outcomes, just as they have so carefully documented crises and disasters. If they are to be the institutions that collectively bring disparate resources together, they must demonstrate to the public that our fight can be won. Like so many of humanity's challenges, this one requires the cohesion that derives from team-building. And we don't have time to argue about it.

Fortunately, as Koebner documents, the world's best zoos have learned to work together. It wasn't always thus. If we are less competitive and more cooperative today, it is because we recognized in our industry's history a dismal conservation record. Recent successes in captive propagation and in situ (field) conservation are the direct result of improvements in communication, technology and population management. It is also clearly the result of an infusion of new talent, bright young scholars and practitioners who have entered the profession that has come to be known as "zoo biology." As this trend continues, zoos and aquariums will become recognized as environmental problem solvers on a global scale. This specialized workforce must grow to meet the challenge.

To succeed, the zoo world must enlist every available resource. By carefully orchestrating our plan, even the tiniest of zoos will have a role to play. We need every curator and every zoo keeper, and we must organize an army of volunteers and technical partners. We must staff conservation, but we must form meaningful coalitions with governments, universities and other conservation organizations. Following the lead of the esteemed Wildlife Conservation Society, our accredited zoos appear equal to these tasks. As Koebner reveals, conservation has become the first priority of all accredited zoos and aquariums.

To all those who read this book, please remember that it is people like you who must join the battle. There is much that you can do to serve the cause of wildlife conservation. As zoos continue to evolve, there is plenty of room for those who would help design, shape, propel and guide a seaworthy ark. Dear reader, you must now prepare to take action.

Terry L. Maple, Ph.D.

Director, Zoo Atlanta

ANIMAL WELFARE, CONSERVATION AND ZOO ORGANIZATIONS

Partial List

American Association of Zoo Keepers
S.W. Gage Boulevard
Topeka, KS 66606

American Humane Association
9725 East Hampden Avenue
Denver, CO 80231

The American Society for the Prevention of
Cruelty to Animals
441 E. 92nd Street
New York, NY 10128

Animal Welfare Institute
P.O. Box 3650
Washington, D.C. 20007

American Zoo And Aquarium Association
7970 D Old Georgetown Road
Bethesda, MD 20814

Conservation International
1015 18th Street NW
Suite 1000
Washington, D.C. 20036

Fund for Animals
200 West 57th Street
New York, NY 10019

Humane Society of the United States
7000 Professional Drive
Gaithersburg, MD 20879

International Union for the
Conservation of Nature
Avenue du Mont-Blanc
Gland, Switzerland

The Jane Goodall Institute
P.O. Box 599
Ridgefield, CT 06877

National Audubon Society
950 Third Avenue
New York, NY 10020

Natural Resources Defense Council
40 West 20th Street
New York, NY 10011

The Nature Conservancy
1815 N. Lynn Street
Arlington, VA 22209

Trout Unlimited
800 Follin Lane SE
Suite 250
Vienna, VA 22180

Wildlife Conservation Society
185th Street and Southern Boulevard
Bronx, NY 10460

World Wildlife Fund
1250 24th Street NW
Washington, DC 20003

The Wolf Fund
Box 471
Moose, Wyoming 83012

Zoocheck Canada
5334 Yonge Street
Suite 1830
Toronto, Ontario M2N 6M2

Zoo Conservation Outreach Group
c/o Fossil Rim
P.O. Box 2189 Rt. 1, Box 210
Glen Rose, TX 76043

1993 AMERICAN ZOO AND AQUARIUM ASSOCIATION, MEMBER INSTITUTIONS

AZA Institution	Address
ALABAMA	
Montgomery Zoo	Box Zebra, Montgomery, AL 36109
ARIZONA	
Phoenix Zoo	455 N. Galvin Parkway, Phoenix, AZ 85008-3431
Wildlife World Zoo	16501 W. Northern Avenue, Litchfield, AZ 85340
Arizona-Sonora Desert Museum	2021 N. Kinney Road, Tucson, AZ 85743-9719
Reid Park Zoo	1100 S. Randolph Way, Tucson, AZ 85716-5830
ARKANSAS	
Little Rock Zoo	#1 Jonesboro St., Little Rock, AR 72205
CALIFORNIA	
Fresno Zoo	894 W. Belmont Ave., Fresno, CA 93728
Happy Hollow Zoo	1300 Senter Road, San Jose, CA 95112
Micke Grove Zoo	11793 N. Micke Grove Road, Lodi, CA 95240-9499
Los Angeles Zoo	5333 Zoo Drive, Los Angeles, CA 90027
Monterey Bay Aquarium	886 Cannery Row, Monterey, CA 93940-1085
Oakland Zoo	Box 5238, Oakland, CA 94605
The Living Desert	47-900 Portola Ave., Palm Desert, CA 92260
Charles Paddock Zoo	9305 Pismo Street, Atascadero, CA 93422
Sacramento Zoo	3930 W. Land Park Drive, Sacramento, CA 95822-1123
San Diego Wild Animal Park	15500 San Pasqual Valley Rd., Escondido, CA 92027
San Diego Zoo	Box 551, San Diego, CA 92112
Sea World of California	1720 S. Shores Road, San Diego, CA 92109-7995
San Francisco Zoo	1 Zoo Road, San Francisco, CA 94132-1098
Santa Ana Zoo	1801 E. Chestnut Ave., Santa Ana, CA 92701-5001
Santa Barbara Zoo	500 Niños Drive, Santa Barbara, CA 93103-3798
Marine World Africa	Marine World Parkway, Vallejo, CA 94589
COLORADO	
Cheyenne Mountain Zoo	4250 Cheyenne Mt. Zoo Road, Colorado Springs, CO 80906
Denver Zoo	City Park, Denver, CO 80205-4899
Pueblo Zoo	3455 Nuckolls Avenue, Pueblo, CO 81055
CONNECTICUT	
Beardsley Zoo	1875 Noble Avenue, Bridgeport, CT 06610
Mystic Marinelife Aquarium	55 Coogan Boulevard, Mystic, CT 06355-1997

DELAWARE
Brandywine Zoo   1001 N. Park Drive, Wilmington, DE 19802-3801

DISTRICT OF COLUMBIA
National Zoological Park   3000 Connecticut Avenue, NW, Washington, DC 20008

FLORIDA
Jacksonville Zoo   8605 Zoo Road, Jacksonville, FL 32218-5769
Discovery Island   Box 10,000, Lake Buena Vista, FL 32830-1000
Central Florida Zoo   Box 470309, Lake Monroe, FL 32747-0309
Miami Metrozoo   12400 SW 152nd Street, Miami, FL 33177-1499
Parrot Jungle   11000 SW 57th Avenue, Miami, FL 33156-4102
St. Augustine Alligator Farm   Box 9005, St. Augustine, FL 32085-9005
Sea World of Florida   7007 Sea World Drive, Orlando, FL 32821-8097
Busch Gardens   Box 9158, Tampa, FL 33674-9158
Lowry Park Zoo   7530 North Blvd., Tampa, FL 33604-4756
The Zoo   5801 Gulf Breeze Parkway, Gulf Breeze, FL 32561-9551
Dreher Park Zoo   1301 Summit Blvd., W. Palm Beach, FL 33405-3098
Living Seas-WDW Epcot Center   P.O. Box 10,000, Lake Buena Vista, FL 32830

GEORGIA
Zoo Atlanta   800 Cherokee Avenue, SE, Atlanta, GA 30315-1440
St. Catharine's Island   Route 1, Box 207-Z, Midway, GA 31320

HAWAII
Honolulu Zoo   151 Kapahulu Ave., Honolulu, HI 96815
Sea Life Park   Makapuu Point, Walmanalo, HI 96795-1897

ILLINOIS
Miller Park Zoo   1020 S. Morris Avenue, Bloomington, IL 61701-6351
Chicago Zoo-Brookfield   Golf Road, Brookfield, IL 60513
Lincoln Park Zoo   2200 North Cannon Drive, Chicago, IL 60614
John G. Shedd Aquarium   1200 S. Lake Shore Drive, Chicago, IL 60605
Glen Oak Zoo   2218 N. Prospect, Peoria, IL 61603-2193
Henson Robinson Zoo   1100 E. Lake Drive, Springfield, IL 62707-8926

INDIANA
Mesker Park Zoo   2421 Bement Avenue, Evansville, IN 47720-5500
Fort Wayne Children's Zoo   3411 Sherman Blvd., Fort Wayne, IN 46808-1594
Indianapolis Zoo   1200 W. Washington Street,
                                         Indianapolis, IN 46222-4500
Potawatomi Zoo   500 S. Greenlawn Ave., South Bend, IN 46615

IOWA
Blank Park Zoo   7401 SW Ninth Street, Des Moines, IA 50315

KANSAS
Emporia Zoo   Box 928, Emporia, KS 66801-0928

Lee Richardson Zoo	Box 499, Garden City, KS 67846-0499
Sunset Zoological Park	2333 Oak Street, Manhattan, KS 66502-3824
Topeka Zoo	635 Gage Blvd., Topeka, KS 66606-2066
Sedgwick County Zoo	5555 Zoo Blvd., Wichita, KS 67212-1643

KENTUCKY
Louisville Zoo	Box 37250, Louisville, KY 40233-7250

LOUISIANA
Alexandria Zoo	Box 71, Alexandria, LA 71309
Greater Baton Rouge Zoo	Box 60, Baker, LA 70704
Audubon Park & Zoo	1140 Seventh Street, New Orleans, LA 70115
Aquarium of the Americas	P.O. Box 4327, New Orleans, LA 70178

MARYLAND
Baltimore Zoo	Druid Hill Park, Baltimore, MD 21217-4900
National Aquarium in Baltimore	Pier 3, 501 E. Pratt Street, Baltimore, MD 21202-3194
Salisbury Zoo	Box 3163, Salisbury, MD 21802

MASSACHUSETTS
New England Aquarium	Central Warf, Boston, MA 02110

MICHIGAN
Binder Park Zoo	7400 Division Road, Battle Creek, MI 49017-9500
Belle Isle Zoo	c/o Detroit Zoo, Box 39, Royal Oak, MI 07652-5392
Detroit Zoo	Box 39, Royal Oak, MI 07652-5392
John Ball Zoo	1300 W. Fulton Street, NW Grand Rapids, MI 49504-6100
Potter Park Zoo	1301 S. Pennsylvania Avenue, Lansing, MI 48912

MINNESOTA
Dickerson Park Zoo	3043 North Fort, Springfield, MO 65803
Minnesota Zoo	13000 Zoo Blvd., Apple Valley, MN 55124-8199
Lake Superior Zoo	7210 Fremont Street, Duluth, MN 55807-1854
St. Paul's Como Zoo	Midway Parkway & Kaufman Drive, St. Paul, MN 55103

MISSISSIPPI
Jackson Zoo	2918 W. Capitol Street, Jackson, MS 39209

MISSOURI
Kansas City Zoo	6700 Zoo Drive, Kansas City, MO 64132
St. Louis Zoo	Forest Park, St. Louis, MO 63110
Dickerson Park Zoo	3043 N. Fort, Springfield, MO 65803

NEBRASKA
Folsom Children's Zoo	1222 South 27th Street, Lincoln, NE 68502
Omaha's Henry Doorly Zoo	3701 S. 10th Street, Omaha, NE 68107-2200
Riverside Zoo	1600 S. Beltline Hwy., Scottsbluff, NE 69361

NEW JERSEY
Bergen County Zoo	216 Forest Avenue, Paramus, NJ 07652-5392
Cape May County Zoo	Route 9 & Pine Lane, Cape May Court House, NJ 08210
New Jersey State Aquarium	1 Riverside Drive, Camden, NJ 08103

NEW MEXICO
Rio Grande Zoo	903 Tenth Street, SW Albuquerque, NM 87102

NEW YORK
Ross Park Zoo	185 Park Avenue, Binghampton, NY 13903
Buffalo Zoo	Delaware Park, Buffalo, NY 14214-9983
Aquarium for Wildlife Cons.	Boardwalk & W. 8th Street, Brooklyn, NY 11224
Int'l Wildlife Conservation Park	185th Street & Southern Blvd., Bronx, NY 10460-1099
Central Park Zoo	830 Fifth Avenue, New York, NY 10021-7095
Staten Island Zoo	614 Broadway, Staten Island, NY 10310
Seneca Park Zoo	2222 St. Paul Street, Rochester, NY 14621-1096
Burnet Park Zoo	500 Burnet Park Drive, Syracuse, NY 13204-2504
Utica Zoo	Steele Hill Road, Utica, NY 13501
Trevor Zoo	Millbrook School Road, Millbrook, NY 12545-9797
Queens Wildlife Center	53-51 111th Street, Flushing, NY 11368

NORTH CAROLINA
North Carolina Zoo	4401 Zoo Parkway, Asheboro, NC 27203-9416
North Carolina Aquariums	417 North Blount Street, Raleigh, NC 27601

NORTH DAKOTA
North Dakota Zoo	P.O. Box 711, Bismark, ND 58502
Roosevelt Park Zoo	Box 538, Minot, ND 58702-0538

OHIO
Sea World	1100 Sea World Drive, Aurora, OH 44202
Cincinnati Zoo	3400 Vine Street, Cincinnati, OH 45220
Cleveland Metroparks Zoo	3900 Brookside Park Drive, Cleveland, OH 44109
Columbus Zoo	Box 400, Powell, OH 43065-0400
Toledo Zoo	Box 4010, Toledo, OH 43609
Akron Zoo	500 Edgewood Drive, Akron, OH 44307-2199
Wild Animal Habitat	6300 Kings Island Drive, Kings Island, OH 45304-0908

OKLAHOMA
Oklahoma City Zoo	2101 NE 50th Street, Oklahoma City, OK 73111-7199
Tulsa Zoo	5701 E. 36th Street, North Tulsa, OK 74115

OREGON
Washington Park Zoo	4001 SW Canyon Road, Portland, OR 97221-2799
Wildlife Safari	Box 1600, Winston, OR 97496-0231

PENNSYLVANIA
Clyde Peeling's Reptileland	RD 1, Box 388, Allenwood, PA 17810

Erie Zoo	Box 3268, Erie, PA 16508-0268
ZooAmerica-Hersheypark	100 W. Hersheypark Drive, Hershey, PA
Philadelphia Zoo	3400 W. Girard Ave., Philadelphia, PA 19104-1196
Pittsburgh Aviary	Allegheny Commons West, Pittsburgh, PA 15212
Pittsburgh Zoo	Box 5250, Pittsburgh, PA 15206-0250

RHODE ISLAND

Roger Williams Park Zoo	1000 Elmwood Ave., Providence RI 02907-3600

SOUTH CAROLINA

Riverbanks Zoo	Box 1060, Columbia, SC 29202-1060
Greenville Zoo	150 Cleveland Park Drive, Greenville, SC 29601
Brookgreen Gardens	1931 Brookgreen Gardens Drive, Murrells Inlet, SC

SOUTH DAKOTA

Great Plains Zoo	805 South Kiwanis Avenue, Sioux Falls, SD 57104
Bramble Park Zoo	P.O. Box 910, Watertown, SD 57201

TENNESSEE

Grassmere Wildlife Park	P.O. Box 40266, Nashville, TN 37204
Knoxville Zoo	Box 6040, Knoxville, TN 37914
Tennessee Aquarium	P.O. Box 11048, Chattanooga, TN 37401
Memphis Zoo & Aquarium	2000 Galloway Ave., Memphis, TN 38112-9990

TEXAS

Texas Abilene Zoo	Box 60, Abilene, TX 79604
Gladys Porter Zoo	500 Ringgold Street, Brownsville, TX 78520
Dallas Zoo	621 E. Clarendon Drive, Dallas, TX 75203-2996
El Paso Zoo	4001 E. Paisano, El Paso, TX 79905-4223
Fort Worth Zoo	1989 Colonial Parkway, Fort Worth, TX 76110-1797
Fossil Rim Wildlife Center	Box 2189, Glen Rose, TX 76043-9729
Houston Zoo	1513 N. MacGregor, Houston, TX 77030
Ellen Trout Zoo	402 Zoo Circle, Lufkin, TX 75901
Sea World	10500 Sea World Drive, San Antonio, TX 78251
San Antonio Zoo & Aquarium	3903 N. St. Mary's Street, San Antonio, TX 78212-3199
Caldwell Zoo	Box 4280, Tyler, TX 75712
The Texas Zoo	Box 69, Victoria, TX 77902-0069
Cameron Park Zoo	Route 10, Box 173-E, Waco, TX 76708

UTAH

Tracy Aviary	589 East 1300 South, Salt Lake City, UT 84105
Hogle Zoo	Box 58475, Salt Lake City, UT 84108-0475

VIRGINIA

National Zoological Park	
C&R Center	1500 Remount Road, Front Royal, VA 22630
Virginia Zoo	3500 Granby Street, Norfolk, VA 23504

WASHINGTON

The Seattle Aquarium	1483 Alaskan Way, Pier 59, Waterfront Pk, Seattle, WA 98101
Woodland Park Zoo	5500 Phinney Ave., North Seattle, WA 98103-5897
Northwest Trek Wildlife Park	11610 Trek Drive East, Eatonville, WA 98328
Point Defiance Zoo	5400 North Pearl Street, Tacoma, WA 98407-3218

WEST VIRGINIA

Oglebay's Good Children's Zoo	Oglebay Park, Wheeling, WV 26003

WISCONSIN

Henry Villas Zoo	702 S. Randall Avenue, Madison, WI 53715-1665
International Crane Foundation	E-11376 Shady Lane Road, Baraboo, WI 53913
Milwaukee County Zoo	10001 W. Bluemound Rd., Milwaukee, WI 53226-4384
Racine Zoo	2131 N. Main Street, Racine, WI 53402-4772

BERMUDA

Bermuda Aquarium	P.O. Box FL 145, Flatts FL BX, Bermuda

DOMINICAN REPUBLIC

Parque Zoological Nacional	ZOODOM P.O. Box 2449, Santo Domingo, Dominican Republic

CANADA

Calgary Zoo	Box 3036, Station B, Calgary, Alberta, T2M 4R8 CANADA
Vancouver Aquarium	Box 3232, Vancouver, BC V6B 3X8 CANADA
Jardin Zoologique De Granby	347 Bourget, Granby, Quebec, CANADA J2G 1E8
Metro Toronto Zoo	P.O. Box 280, West Hill, Toronto, CANADA M1E 4R5

GLOSSARY

ACCREDITED (as in zoos:) Those having met the strict standards of the American Zoo and Aquarium Association (AZA).

ANIMAL KEEPER: A person responsible for the daily care and well-being of a captive animal.

ANIMAL RECORD KEEPING SYSTEM (ARKS): A computer program used by 350 animal facilities worldwide to collect and distribute information about individual animals.

ANIMAL WELFARE ORGANIZA-TIONS: Not-for-profit organization devoted to the preservation and well-being of animals.

ANTHROPOLOGY: The study of the different cultures, customs, and behaviors of human beings.

THE AMERICAN ZOO AND AQUARIUM ASSOCIATION (AZA): The national membership organization for accredited zoos and zoo professionals.

BIODIVERSITY: The diversity of all living things (species) and of life patterns and processes (ecosystem structure and functions), including genetic diversity, species and population diversity, ecosystem diversity, landscape and regional diversity, and biosphere diversity.

BIOTELEMETRY: The remote sensing and measuring of biological functions of living things.

BOTANIST: A person who specializes in the study of plants.

BRACHIATE: To swing by the arms from object to object (branch to branch or bars on a jungle gym) the way some apes do.

BUSHMEAT: The meat of wild animals either killed or scavenged by humans for food.

CAPTIVE BREEDING SPECIALIST GROUP (CBSG): Professionals who make recommendations.

CAPTIVITY: Being confined, not free.

CARRION: Dead and decaying flesh.

CLEAR CUTTING: Indiscriminately cutting forests, leaving open fields.

CONVENTION ON INTERNATIONAL TRADE IN ENDANGERED SPECIES (CITIES): Created in 1973, an agreement signed by over 100 countries not to exploit international wildlife. The result of a desire to regulate and control the market in wild animals and plants.

CRYOGENICS: Freezing genetic material at very cold temperatures (-196° C) for future use and research.

CURATOR: A manager or director.

DART GUN: A gun which fires darts filled with medication in order to anesthetize or treat an animal.

DARWINISM: The evolutionary concept first proposed by Charles Darwin that evolution proceeds through the survival for the best adapted individual of a particular species.

DOCENT: A volunteer at zoos who helps teach visitors about the animals, exhibits, and conservation issues.

ECOLOGIST: A scientist who studies ecosystems.

ECOSYSTEM: A community of all the plants and animals in an area together with the physical environment and how they function as a whole.

EMBRYO TRANSFER: Transplanting the embryo of an endangered animal into a compatible female of the same family, but less rare animal (e.g. guar embryo into a cow). This technique allows more animals of an endangered species to be born, with less risk to the female of the endangered species.

ENDANGERED SPECIES: Animal or plant species in danger of becoming extinct.

ENDANGERED SPECIES ACT: A law passed by the United States Congress to identify and help protect endangered species.

ENRICHMENT: Providing activities and objects to enhance an environment and make the daily activity of an animal fuller and more meaningful.

EPIDEMIC: A contagious disease that spreads rapidly and extensively among many individuals in an area.

ETHICS: The study of morals and the basis for making choices.

ETHOLOGIST: A scientist who studies the natural behavior of animals.

EX SITU: Out of/away from the natural habitat.

EXTINCTION: No longer existing; every one of a certain species or group being dead.

FAUNA: Usually refers to all of the animals of a particular region or area.

FAUNAL INTEREST GROUP (FIG): An organized committee of individuals in and out of the zoo that make recommendations about the management of the wildlife, plants, and reserves in entire areas of the world. Currently there are FIGs for Madagascar, Southeast Asia, Brazil, Zaire, and the West Indies.

FLIGHT CAGE: A very large aviary. An enclosed space, large enough for birds to have free flight, in a naturalistic habitat.

FLORA: Usually refers to all the plants of a particular region or area.

FOUNDER ANIMALS: Unrelated individuals of a species on which a captive population is established.

FRAGMENTATION: Populations separated into small groups.

GAMETES: Mature egg or sperm capable of participating in fertilization.

GENE MAPPING: The process of locating individual genes within the chromosome responsible for the genetic transmission of specific traits.

GENE POOL: The total number and variety of genes in a given population.

GENETICIST: A scientist who studies genes and genetics.

GORILLA TROOP: A group of gorillas, usually comprised of an adult male (silverback), adolescent males and females, several adult females, and their offspring. They function as a community.

HERPETOLOGY: The scientific study of reptiles and amphibians.

HOOF STOCK: Referring to animals with horny covering protecting the toes or encasing the foot.

HORTICULTURIST: An expert in the science and art of cultivating plants.

ICHTHYOLOGY: The study of fish.

IN SITU: In (its original) place.

IN VITRO: In an artificial environment outside the living organism.

INBREEDING: The continued multigenerational breeding of closely related individuals.

INDIGENOUS: Born or growing naturally in a region or country; native.

INTERNATIONAL UNION OF DIRECTORS OF ZOOLOGICAL PARKS: The organized committee of zoo directors from accredited facilities worldwide.

INTERNATIONAL SPECIES INVENTORY SYSTEM (ISIS): A data bank of information on individual captive species and their ancestors in the world's participating zoos. Founded in 1974.

INVERTEBRATE: Animals without a backbone, such as insects, jellyfish, and crabs.

KEYSTONE SPECIES: An animal that is important in the ecosystem, and that other animals are dependent upon.

LANDSCAPE IMMERSION: Terminology for exhibits that make the visitor feel that they are in the habitat along with the plants and animals.

MAMMOLOGY: The study of mammals.

MENAGERIE: A random grouping of wild animals for exhibition with little planning for their care or housing.

NATURAL HABITATS: A naturally occurring or recreated area or type of environment in which an organism or biological population usually lives or occurs.

NATURALISTIC EXHIBITS: Animal enclosures and exhibits which recreate the animals' natural habitat.

NOCTURNAL: Active at night.

ORNITHOLOGY: The scientific study of birds.

POLE SYRINGE: A syringe on a pole used to medicate an animal.

POSTAGE STAMP COLLECTION: Referring to captive animals caged individually. Many different species housed next to one another with no plan, attention to the needs of the animal, or educational purpose.

POTENTATE: A monarch, a leader of groups and endeavors.

RADIO TELEMETRY: Tracking animals with a radio transmitter, thereby being able to know where they are at long distances when they are not in sight.

RESTORATION ECOLOGY: Repairing entire ecosystems.

ROBO-BADGER: The nickname for a mechanical badger, which was designed to teach captive black-footed ferrets to be afraid of their natural predators before being released into the wild.

SINGLE POPULATION ANALYSIS AND RECORD KEEPING SYSTEM (SPARKS): Computer software to analyze demographics and genetics to manage species more efficiently.

SISTER ZOO: A zoo in Central America with a relationship to a North American zoo.

STEREOTYPE: An excessive repetition of behavior.

TAXON ADVISORY GROUP: A group of individuals who evaluate and recommend solutions for entire taxa, or groups of animals.

TOUCH TABLES: Places for zoo visitors to examine artifacts.

TRANSLOCATION: Moving to another location.

THREATENED: A species at risk of extinction, but not yet endangered.

TRANSPONDER: A computer tag that records detailed information.

ZOO: An abbreviation for Zoological Park or Zoological Garden. A park or facility where exotic animals are kept for the purpose of conservation, education, and recreation. The *Oxford English Dictionary* gives 1847 as the date the word "zoo" was first used.

ZOOGEOGRAPHIC: Animals of a particular geographic region.

PHOTO CREDITS

Coleman, Inc.

99 top: Collecting data from a walrus
© Chicago Zoological Society

99 middle: Inobtrusive method
© Jon Coe

99 bottom: Two methods for drawing blood
© Jon Coe

100 Two baby orangutans
© Zoological Society of San Diego, photo by Ron Garrison

101 top: Orangutan
© Zoological Society of San Diego, photo by Ron Garrison

101 middle: Baby aardvark
© Zoological Society of San Diego

101 bottom: Two baby tamarins
© Pauline R. McCann/Bruce Coleman, Inc.

102 top: Baby tiger
© NYZS/The Wildlife Conservation Society

102 middle: Baby hippopotamus
© NYZS/The Wildlife Conservation Society, D. DeMello

102 bottom: Two baby chimpanzees
© Linda Koebner

103 top: Volunteer and children
© The Lincoln Park Zoological Society/Susie Reich

103 bottom: Volunteers at Zoo Atlanta teach
© Michael K. Nichols, Magnum

104 Bushmaster gets fed
© Michael K. Nichols, Magnum

106 Food preparation
© Joe Sebo/Zoo Atlanta

107 Commissary food
© Linda Koebner/Bruce Coleman, Inc.

108 top: Kevin Bell
© Lincoln Park Zoological Society/Cathy Bell

108 middle: William Conway
© Michael K. Nichols, Magnum

108 bottom: L. Ronald Forman
© Audubon Institute/Mike DeMocker

109 top: David Hancocks
© Michael R. Stoklos

109 bottom: Palmer Krantz
© Riverbanks Zoological Park

110 top: Terry Maple
Courtesy Zoo Atlanta

110 bottom: Thomas Otten
Courtesy Point Defiance Zoo and Aquarium

111 top: George Rabb

© Chicago Zoological Society, photo by Jim Schulz

111 bottom: Y. Sherry Sheng
© Washington Park Zoo/Michael Durham

112 Patricia Simmons
Courtesy Akron Zoo

113 top: John Coe
© Gail Hern

113 bottom: Giraffe
© Jerry Howard

115 Joan Embry
© Zoological Society of San Diego

CHAPTER 6

117 Zebras
© The Telegraph Colour Library/FPG International

120 The graveyard at the Bronx Zoo
© NYZS/The Wildlife Conservation Society

121 Elephant
© K. Ammann/Bruce Coleman, Inc.

122 Douglas Hamilton
© NYZS/The Wildlife Conservation Society

123 top: Rhino horn daggers
© NYZS/The Wildlife Conservation Society/Philip Crayford

123 bottom: Ivory storehouse
© NYZS/The Wildlife Conservation Society

124 Rondonia, Brazil
Michael K. Nichols, Magnum

CHAPTER 7

127 Lowland gorilla Jessica with baby
© Zoological Society of San Diego, photo by Ron Garrison

128 Snow leopard
© Rod Williams/Bruce Coleman, Inc.

130 Siberian tiger mother with cubs
© The Telegraph Colour Library/FPG International

132 Snow leopard cubs
© Whittaker/Lane Agency/Bruce Coleman, Inc.

133 Female gerenuks
© K. & K. Ammann/Bruce Coleman, Inc.

134 Dr. Betsy Dresser
Courtesy Cincinnati Zoo and Botanical Garden, photo by Steve Feist

135 A bongo calf born to an eland
Courtesy Cincinnati Zoo and Botanical Garden

136 Artificial egg
© NYZS/The Wildlife Conservation Society, Bill Meng

137 White-naped cranes
© NYZS/The Wildlife Conservation Society, D. DeMello

CHAPTER 8

139 Dee Boersma
© NYZS/The WildlifeConservation Society, David Mleczko

140 top: Forest elephants in dense growth
© NYZS/The Wildlife Conservation Society

140 bottom: Keeper and elephant
© NYZS/The Wildlife Conservation Society

141 Baboons
© International Stock/Maratea

142 top: Terese Hart
© NYZS/The Wildlife Conservation Society, John Hart

142 bottom: Wildlife Conservation Society Map
© NYZS/The Wildlife Conservation Society

143 George Schaller
© NYZS/The Wildlife Conservation Society, W. Anway

144 Giant panda
© Michael George/Bruce Coleman, Inc.

145 Alan Rabinowitz
© NYZS/The Wildlife Conservation Society, B. Campbell

146 Amy Vedder
© NYZS/The Wildlife Conservation Society, Bill Weber

147 Baby mountain gorilla
© Animals Animals/Bruce Davidson

148 Scarlet and green macaws
© NYZS/The Wildlife Conservation Society, Charles Munn

149 Charles Munn
© NYZS/The Wildlife Conservation Society, Mary Helsaple

150 Airlift
© Fred Koontz

151 top: Rhino management
© N. Myers/Bruce Coleman, Inc.

151 bottom: Two rhinos
© Patricia D. Moehlman

CHAPTER 9

153 Arabian oryx
© NYZS/The Wildlife Conservation Society

154 Aruba Island rattlesnake
© Zoological Society of San

Diego

155 Bali mynah
© Kennth W. Fink/Bruce Coleman, Inc.

157 Golden lion tamarin
© Kenneth W. Fink/Bruce Coleman, Inc.

159 Black-footed ferret
Photo by LuRay Parker/© 1985 Wyoming Game & Fish Dept.

161 top: California condor
© Mike Wallace/Courtesy LA Zoo

162 Adult condor
© Mike Wallace/Courtesy LA Zoo

161 bottom: Puppet and chick–California condor
© Mike Wallace/Courtesy LA Zoo

CHAPTER 10

164 Leopard in cage
© JC Carton/Bruce Coleman, Inc.

164 Orangutan behind bars
© Gary R. Zahm/Bruce Coleman, Inc.

166 A roadside menagerie
© Jessica Ehlers/Bruce Coleman, Inc.

CHAPTER 11

173 Buffalo
© 1988, Richard Biegum, FPG International

MISCELLANEOUS

8 Elephants at Busch Gardens
© Michael K. Nichols, Magnum

11 Gibbons in JungleWorld
© NYZS/The Wildlife Conservation Society

14 Gerenuk
© K. Ammann/Bruce Coleman, Inc.

16 Proboscis monkeys in JungleWorld Exhibit
© Michael K. Nichols, Magnum

17 Gharial crocodiles in JungleWorld
© Michael K. Nichols, Magnum

19 Rhino and sable
© Zoological Society of San Diego, photo by Ron Garrison

20 Cupid the hippo at Toledo Zoo
© Michael K. Nichols, Magnum

21 Przewalski horse at Front Royal National Zoo
© 1988, Kenneth Garrett/FPG International